ただきます

'ANY SUFFICIENTLY ~~ADVANCED TECHNOLOGY~~
DELICIOUS INGREDIENT IS INDISTINGUISHABLE FROM MAGIC.'

ARTHUR C. CLARKE

FOR FELIX

NOTHING MAKES ME PROUDER
THAN MAKING THINGS
YOU LOVE TO EAT

JAPANEASY KITCHEN

TIM ANDERSON

SIMPLE RECIPES USING JAPANESE PANTRY INGREDIENTS

PHOTOGRAPHY BY PATRICIA NIVEN

Quadrille

INTRODUCTION

DISCLAIMER

**THIS IS NOT A JAPANESE COOKBOOK.
I MEAN, IT IS . . . BUT MOSTLY, IT ISN'T.**

It would make sense to put this book on the Japanese shelf in a bookshop, that is true. And calling it *JapanEasy* is probably not too misleading. But most of the recipes themselves are not Japanese.

Let me explain: this is a Japanese cookbook in the sense that its focus is on Japanese ingredients and flavours, but not necessarily in Japanese dishes. Which is okay! You don't have to relegate Japanese ingredients to Japanese cuisine. In fact, you *shouldn't* do that! Because they really are magical. They have the power to utterly transform your food.

But of course, simply using Japanese ingredients doesn't make your cooking Japanese. Hence this disclaimer – I want to be abundantly clear. A few years ago, it occurred to me that some people might own just one Japanese cookbook, and that cookbook might be one that I've written. I'm grateful for this, but it's also kind of horrifying. Japanese cooking is an ENORMOUS topic – it never ends, and I mean that literally. It grows, changes and expands like the universe, forever. And it's not my place – nor anybody's, but *definitely* not mine – to be the sole arbiter of information on Japanese food, even in just one person's home.

So I feel duty-bound to inform you when I'm stepping outside the established borders of Japanese food. This is something I do every day in my own kitchen, and it doesn't really matter. But when it's in a book, there's a real risk of misrepresentation, and people getting the wrong idea. *So don't get the wrong idea!*

Lately, I've been thinking about something the Kurdish food writer Melek Erdal wrote in *Vittles*:

> '*It's my culture, I'm allowed to disrespect it* ... Who has the right to deviate from an original recipe, how and why? Aren't all recipes deviations from ones that preceeded them? I was once asked, "What is Kurdish food?", and my response was, "Anything I make."'

As Chris Hemsworth said in Taika Waititi's classic *Thor: Ragnarok*, 'Asgard is not a place. It's a people.' Erdal's culture and her food are embodied in her and her community, wherever they stand. She can alter traditional dishes as she sees fit, operating within an understanding of their history and significance. She knows where the boundaries are, and which ones can't be crossed. And she can justify adaptations for all sorts of legitimate reasons – or she can choose not to justify them if she doesn't want to. She doesn't have to! It's *her* food.

Years ago, I read an online review of one of my books that I still think about, because it was so inescapably, brutally true. The headline read: 'White people Japanese food.' The gist of the review itself was exactly that: not that the recipes were inauthentic or inaccurate per se, but they were clearly curated by a white person, writing for a mostly white audience, in a way that would be palatable and accessible to them.

The cleverest thing about this review is that it would be true *no matter what*. Whatever dishes I choose, and however I present or adapt them, they'll inevitably be filtered and refracted through my own perspective and experience as an American (and reluctantly British) white dude. Even if I make a conscious effort to represent dishes and aspects of Japanese culture as faithfully as possible, it's still *white people Japanese food*, because it's Japanese food for white people, i.e., me. Wherever you go, there you are.

But at this point, Japanese food is simply the food I'm most familiar with – even more so than the American food I grew up eating. Whenever I cook food from Wisconsin, I have to look up recipes online and familiarise myself with unusual American seasonings. (Like celery salt – what the heck!?)

Cooking Japanese food comes naturally because I've spent a long time doing it. Making Japanese food as a matter of routine has a lot to do with understanding Japanese seasonings. And those seasonings end up in all of my cooking – not just Japanese. Chilli con carne needs a little depth? *Tamari*. Bechamel too bland? *White miso*. Salad dressing too sharp? *Mirin*. Using these ingredients is second nature. Hell, it's first nature. It's just how I cook, and my cooking's better for it. And yours can be, too!

Japanese ingredients are magic, capable of changing up dishes in ways that can be subtle or spectactular. There are no limits to what you can do with them. So maybe this isn't a Japanese cookbook, but instead, think of it as a Japanese culinary workbook. 'A dash of this, a dash of that' cooking comes with time and practise, and these recipes will help you develop those intuitive seasoning skills. And, as a bonus, they're *really* delicious – and really easy, of course!

THE F WORD

Most of the recipes in this book could be described as 'Japanese fusion'. I didn't intend to write recipes like this from the outset. I intended to answer the question: 'I have some [insert Japanese ingredient here] – what can I do with it?'

The obvious answer, of course, is: cook Japanese food! There are lots of books that can help with that, but that's not what's really being asked. Really, the question is: what else can I do with it? How can I use it in other types of cooking and incorporate it into my daily repertoire? The answer to *that* question is, in a nutshell: *fusion*.

I want to break down what that means, because fusion can be something of a dirty word. This is partly because a lot of fusion food just isn't very good – it's not an improvement on the source material. But it's also because of fusion's problematic history.

Jenny Lau, in her indispensible *An A–Z of Chinese Food*, lays out this history, taking it back to the 1980s. Lau assesses that Wolfgang Puck's first Asian fusion restaurant, Chinois, initiated the ongoing trend of fusion food as a commercial concept. The Puck school of fusion, Lau says, is a form of cultural appropriation 'where a chef from a dominant culture cherry-picks elements of Asia's vast and expansive cuisines – exclusively those elements that are most exciting and exotic yet palatable enough to enhance their menu ... with hardly any reciprocal benefit to the cultures that are being pillaged.'

Lau calls this 'graft-chimera' fusion rather than a true hybrid, a lopsided, superficial and self-serving endeavour whose perpetrators aren't involved in the groundwork of supporting the cultures from which they're taking. In a previous book, I described this (with far less eloquence) as 'stupid fusion': the mindless smashing together of two different cuisines, like a caveman hitting rocks together in attempts to make fire or entertain himself. This is distinct from the kind of natural fusion derived from the movement of people as they encounter new territories and societies, adapting and innovating as they go.

However, fusion food doesn't always fall neatly into one of these two categories. Take the Korean taco. The Korean taco is a product of genuine love, familiarity and respect for the Los Angeles subcultures that inspired it. It would be absurd to accuse its creators, Roy Choi and Mark Manguera, of appropriation. But the Korean taco was also a commercial prospect, the brainchild of two creative entrepreneurs who saw a gap in the market. It had no real precedent among the Korean and Mexican diaspora communities of LA.

Another case in point: katsu curry. The UK has gone katsu curry crazy, and we've taken the dish in directions that might be seen as pretty bizarre in Japan – like katsu curry-flavoured cheese, katsu curry baby food and the katsu curry bake at the British bakery chain Gregg's (all actual items). But katsu curry's roots are, in fact, British. Japan adopted curry from British sources in the late 19th century, when it had already been warped into something completely different from its South Asian origins.

So what do we make of things like Gregg's katsu curry bake and the Korean taco? Are they cash-grabbing graft-chimeras? Or true hybrids that blossom in the borderlands between cultures? I think they're kind of both – and that's why they work. They speak to a specific locality and moment in history. The Korean taco tastes like Los Angeles; the katsu curry bake tastes like, I don't know, Middlesbrough or something.

In nature, true genetic chimeras do exist, and they're often mesmerising, simultaneously strange and beautiful. Look up half-sider budgerigars, African violet chimeras and gynandomorphic butterflies and you'll see what I mean. My point is that there are many different modes of fusion: good, bad, ugly, beautiful, natural and unnatural. Fusion is a complex topic, and while many of us – myself included – feel uncomfortable with the term and indeed the whole concept, it isn't always illegitimate. But the who, where, why and how of it all are always worth considering. Where do culinary tourists and magpies like David Chang or Rick Stein or Yotam Ottolenghi fit into all of this? Where do I fit in? Where do *you* fit in?

Well, that's an easy one: where you fit in is your own home kitchen. And nobody really cares what you get up to in there. But spare a thought for the origins of all the incredible international ingredients we now have access to. Locate them within the space-time-culture continuum before you put them on your eggs. Ask yourself: does this make sense, or am I just smashing rocks together?

In *Small Fires*, Rebecca May Johnson describes recipes as 'capacious', accommodating thousands of variations depending on who cooks it and how they cook them. 'Broad reception enriches rather than impoverishes the recipe by giving many hands the power of transformation,' Johnson writes. I feel similarly about ingredients. Calling forth your soy sauce, miso, mirin etc. to use in non-Japanese dishes does not diminish them – quite the contrary, only relegating them to the back of the cupboard would do that. To take them into new frontiers is to expand their power. So use them, respect them – and have fun with them!

Clearspring
S&B
GOLDEN CURRY
JAPANESE CURRY MIX
Clearspring
TOFU
タマノイ
米酢
Gluten Free
国産米100%
本みりん
醤油こうじ
料理酒
醸造調味料
国産米使用
KIKKOMAN
とうふのみそ汁
INSTANT TOFU MISO SOUP

KNOWING MISO, KNOWING SHŌYU

JAPANESE STORECUPBOARD STAPLES: A BRIEF INTRODUCTION

Right, with all of that in mind, let's talk about which ingredients, exactly, we're dealing with. Allow me to introduce the FAB, uh ... NINE! Nine categories of ingredients around which this book is structured:

1. **KOMBU AND KATSUOBUSHI**
2. **MISO**
3. **SOY SAUCE**
4. **SAKE, MIRIN AND RICE VINEGAR**
5. **RICE AND NOODLES**
6. **TOFU**
7. **PONZU, YUZU JUICE AND YUZU KOSHŌ**
8. **CURRY ROUX**
9. **TEA AND OTHER BEVERAGES**

You won't need all of these all of the time, but there's a lot of overlap between chapters. Besides, these are some of the most versatile, delicious ingredients in the world, so it's a good idea to have a wide range of them to hand. They don't really go off and you'll get through them anyway (with a little help from this book!).

Each chapter has an introduction to each ingredient (or set of ingredients), including a brief history and shopping guide. As a general rule, **when you're cooking Japanese food**, *use Japanese ingredients!* That may go without saying, but I often find home cooks and even professional chefs attempting Japanese food with ingredients from elsewhere in East Asia, and frankly the results are embarrassing. The flavour of Japanese *shōyu* (soy sauce) is simply not the same as Chinese *jiàngyóu*. I've nothing against the rest of Asia, of course! It's just that non-Japanese ingredients don't taste right in Japanese food. Besides, all of these recipes were tested with Japanese ingredients, not their continental counterparts. I don't know if they'll even work.

There are, however, some cases where Chinese or Korean equivalents are perfectly fine to use: namely, sesame seeds and sesame oil. But whatever you do, DO NOT SERVE JAPANESE FOOD WITH LONG-GRAIN RICE. It's just plain weird!

Many recipes call for Japanese ingredients beyond these main categories. Here's a brief explanation of others you'll encounter:

DASHI POWDER (DASHI NO MOTO / 出汁の素)

Instant Japanese soup powder. The two most common types are kombu (kelp) and katsuo (smoked fish). Where no specific type is indicated, either will do.

MSG (AJINOMOTO / 味の素 OR UMAMI CHŌMIRYŌ / うま味調味料)

If you're still weird about MSG, please educate yourself. It's fine – and delicious.

SESAME SEEDS (GOMA / 胡麻) AND SESAME OIL (GOMA ABURA / 胡麻油)

Must always be toasted. Chinese and Korean versions are just as good.

SHICHIMI

Shorthand for SHICHIMI TŌGARASHI (七味唐辛子), a seven-spice blend which is predominantly chilli powder, along with other aromatics including orange peel, sesame seeds and nori.

SANSHŌ (山椒)

The Japanese cultivar of Sichuan pepper. Milder in flavour, with an uplifting lemongrass-like aroma and a slight tingle. Choose sanshō that looks olive to lime green in colour; dark green sanshō powders have been ground together with their black seeds, which are flavourless and gritty.

AONORI (青のり)

Green seaweed flakes, used as a garnish or seasoning.

JAPANESE MUSTARD

A hot, punchy mustard called KARASHI (からし) or WAGARASHI (和がらし), sold in little tubes like wasabi. Prepared English mustard makes a fine substitute.

UMEBOSHI (梅干し)

Intensely sour and salty pickled plums.

YUKARI (ゆかり)

Furikake (rice seasoning) made from dried purple shiso, a fragrant Japanese herb.

みたけ
SHICHIMI TOGARASHI
おいしい梅干
oishii umeboshi
NAKATA FOODS
mishima
ゆかり
NET WT.
40g
8bags×5g
SATISFACTION
シマヤだしの素
DASHI-NO-MOTO
JAPANESE TRADITIONAL SOUP STOCK

WASABI (わさび)

For these recipes, there's no need to splurge on anything other than the basic stuff from a tube. But avoid wasabi powder, as it tends to be quite bitter.

PICKLED GINGER

This is either GARI (ガリ), the thinly sliced, pale pink or yellow sweet pickled ginger used as a palate cleanser for sushi; or BENI SHŌGA (紅生姜), the julienned, red or bright pink kind, which is incorporated into dishes or used as a garnish. Recipes specify which type to use.

NORI (海苔)

Blackish-green seaweed sheets, often used for sushi, but in this book it is mostly used as a garnish, snipped into fine shreds with scissors.

TONKATSU SAUCE (とんかつソース)

Japanese brown sauce, with a sweet and tangy flavour. Common brands are Bulldog and Otafuku.

PANKO (パン粉)

Japanese breadcrumbs, which are airier in texture and more shard-like in shape than regular dried breadcrumbs, allowing for a superlative crunch. If you've got panko left over from panéing, freeze it – you can use it the next time you need to breadcrumb something.

I am often asked: where do you buy Japanese ingredients? My answer is always unsatisfying, because I have no one go-to shop. Instead, I shop around, looking for the best deals and the best variety. I do almost all of my Japanese shopping online, and here in the UK I am able to get everything I need (and then some) through STARRY MART, JAPAN CENTRE, THE WASABI COMPANY, SOUS CHEF and NATURAL NATURAL. Ordinary online supermarkets will also have you covered for most basics. OCADO and WAITROSE consistently have the best ranges. And in a pinch – although I am reluctant to recommend them – Amazon will deliver a lot of Japanese seasonings, too.

As always, SUPPORT YOUR LOCAL ASIAN SUPERMARKET, if you have one. In a time when high street retail is constantly struggling, these shops are invaluable, so use 'em or lose 'em!

FURIKAKE (ふりかけ)

A dry seasoning to sprinkle onto plain rice. There are hundreds of flavours but they are typically based on seaweed or dried fish, so if you're vegan, just make sure to buy vegan versions. Recipes that call for furikake can use any kind, but I recommend the homemade version on page 24.

HOW TO USE THIS BOOK

The recipes here are simple and straightforward, but please read the following notes to make your cooking go as smoothly as possible.

In addition to the nine ingredients-based chapters, there is also an appendix of basic sauces and seasonings that you can use in a wide variety of meals: THE LIBRARY OF CONDIMENTS (pages 187–216). These are essentially various ways you can combine Japanese seasonings to make sauces, dressings, dips, drizzles, marinades, brines, glazes, etc. that can be used on everything from salads to steaks. Often, these are key to making quick Japanese meals on demand.

STAR RECIPES! ✯

This book has a lot of recipes! More than my other cookbooks. This is in order to better showcase the versatility and range of each ingredient. The drawback is that it can make it difficult to choose which recipes to try. I've added a star symbol to the ones I recommend the most. (It turns out that your recipes are like your children, in the sense that it's pretty easy to choose favourites.)

VEGAN THINGS!

While this isn't a vegan cookbook, many of the recipes steer clear of eggs and dairy, because my son is allergic to them. This means that many of the dishes are either naturally vegan, or easily vegan-isable with a few simple swaps. The leaf symbol will tell you when a dish is vegan, or can be made vegan (just look for the note at the bottom of the page for specific instructions to this end). Unless otherwise specified, vegan versions of common pantry ingredients, like Worcestershire sauce, will work perfectly well as substitutes.

As far as vegan dairy products go, I've tested these recipes with a variety of plant milks, creams and butters. I am confident that most brands will work, but I do prefer Oatly cream and Flora plant butter for both consistency and flavour. Plant milks should be unsweetened.

COOK'S NOTES

'OIL' indicates neutral vegetable oil.

'VINEGAR' indicates Japanese rice vinegar.

'SUGAR' indicates white caster (superfine) or granulated sugar unless another kind is specified.

'DASHI' indicates prepared liquid dashi;
'DASHI POWDER' indicates the powder itself.

1 TABLESPOON is 15 ml; 1 TEASPOON is 5 ml.

MEASURE BY VOLUME OR WEIGHT as the recipe indicates.

USE FINE SALT unless sea salt flakes are specified.

JAPANESE NOMENCLATURE 日本語

Primarily to provide a reference for those who are curious, I have included Japanese titles in both Japanese and Roman text for dishes that are traditional or common in Japan. If there's no Japanese, the dish is something I've invented and not part of established Japanese gastronomy (that I know of).

CHAPTER 1

昆布と鰹節

KOMBU & KATSUOBUSHI

We begin with KOMBU (DRIED KELP / 昆布) and KATSUOBUSHI (SMOKED BONITO FLAKES / 鰹節), because in so many ways, that's where Japanese food begins. These are the key ingredients in DASHI (出汁), the soup stock which is light on the palate but rich in umami, and forms one of the key pillars of Japanese flavour.

I read on a packet of Japanese crisps (no joke) that kombu consumption in Japan dates back to the Jōmon period, roughly 10,000 years ago, although some cursory internet research suggests that it was actually wakame seaweed that archaeologists have found among Jōmon ruins. Still, kombu's got a long, long history in Japan – it first appears in writing in the 8th century, but it was almost certainly eaten long before that. Nowadays, kombu is still eaten, in various forms, but it is most commonly used to make dashi. Its umami compounds are off the charts, and it has a briny, oceanic aroma and slight sweetness. It is indispensible.

The kombu you are most likely to find in shops is just... kombu. Basic kombu of no particular designation, and usually not even from Japan. But this stuff is fine – for everyday cooking, it will provide the flavour you're looking for in dashi, and it has an amenable texture for eating, as well. But you may also come across specific varieties of kombu, which have particular properties and come from different regions of Hokkaido, Japan's northernmost island. There are four main designations.

MA KOMBU (真昆布)

Produces a light, versatile dashi that won't overpower even delicate ingredients.

HIDAKA KOMBU (日高昆布)

Soft and tender, so it's great for eating, and quickly relinquishes its flavour to make dashi of moderate intensity.

RISHIRI KOMBU (利尻昆布)

A firm, dark kombu that makes a strong, aromatic and slightly saline dashi that requires more time to infuse. This is my favourite kombu for dashi, but it isn't great for eating, because of its toughness.

RAUSU KOMBU (羅臼昆布)

Produces an intense dashi that works well with other strongly flavoured ingredients, such as beef and soy sauce.

These are just the A-listers, but for the purposes of this book, cheap and cheerful is absolutely fine. In fact, this is preferable in dishes where the kombu is eaten, such as the Spent Dashi Puttanesca (page 25).

Kombu produces tasty dashi on its own, but the signature flavour of smoked fish at the foundation of so much Japanese cooking comes from katsuobushi. *Katsuo* is bonito, and *bushi* (or technically *fushi*) are flakes. So 'bonito flakes' is a perfectly accurate translation, but this belies its complex production process. Dried fish products have been used in Japanese cooking for well over a millennium, but the smoked and fermented katsuobushi we enjoy today is a more recent development, dating back to the Edo period (circa 17th century). At that time, katsuo fishermen in Shikoku and the Kii peninsula discovered that both smoking the fish and inoculating it with kōji helped prevent spoilage as it dried – and enhanced its flavour, too. The finished product is completely desiccated and resembles a piece of wood, which is then shaved on a tool called a kezuriki, which, sure enough, is like an inverted carpenter's plane. The shavings are then infused into dashi, or eaten as a garnish.

Most commercial katsuobushi is what's called ARABUSHI (荒節), literally 'rough shavings', which has been thoroughly smoked and dried, but not inoculated with mould. The pellicle of black smoke particulates that accumulates on the fish is not removed, resulting in a more intense, almost barbecue-like smoky flavour. Katsuobushi that has had its heavily smoked exterior removed is called HADAKABUSHI (裸節) ('naked fushi'), which is less smoky but more fishy. That which has undergone the full process of fermentation and further drying is called HON-KAREBUSHI (本枯節), or just HON-BUSHI (本節), 'true dried fushi'. This dashi is savoury, lightly sweet and comparatively delicate, with a more refined flavour, so it is typically reserved for more subtle styles of cooking, such as *kaiseki*.

As with kombu, you are unlikely to come across anything other than ordinary arabushi, which is usually labelled simply as 'katsuobushi', or sometimes HANA KATSUO (花かつお), or 'flower bonito'. And this stuff is great – as long as it's reasonably fresh. Once shaved, katsuobushi rapidly loses its aroma and begins to oxidise and develop a distinct smell of ammonia, so don't buy anything too close to its use-by date. Once you've opened the bag, the clock is ticking, so keep it sealed tightly and use it up quickly.

Outside Japan, both kombu and katsuobushi are not cheap, so this chapter focuses on uses for them beyond making dashi, so you get more bang for your buck. Many of the recipes are based on a *furikake* (rice seasoning) made from dehydrating the spent ingredients from making dashi. This keeps more or less forever in the cupboard (although it will start to taste a little stale over time), so it's extremely useful. However, I'd also encourage you to try OKAKA (おかか) and TSUKUDANI (佃煮), which preserve spent katsuobushi and kombu, respectively, by braising them in a salty-sweet glaze. Recipes for these can be found in my other books (or all over the internet).

While kombu and katsuobushi are important ingredients to know, you don't have to make dashi from scratch. Dashi from a powder is absolutely fine – cheap, quick and delicious. All of the recipes in this book will be great with instant dashi, but if you make anything where the dashi is front and centre – such as the Kipper Soba (page 112) or Mussel, Wakame and Asparagus Rice Soup (page 106) – consider making your own dashi, to enjoy its refined and rounded flavour.

DASHI THREE WAYS ✯

EACH MAKES ABOUT 500 ML (17 FL OZ/2 CUPS) – ENOUGH FOR 2 BOWLS OF NOODLES

While most dashi recipes call for heating the kombu for various lengths of time, all of these recipes start with a cold infusion. The actual hands-on cooking time is less than five minutes, so they're incredibly easy to make. As easy as instant? Well no, not quite, but homemade dashi is a special, subtle thing, so treat yourself every once in a while.

Dashi is always best freshly made, but it will keep in the refrigerator for one or two days. Anything beyond this will start to taste insipid as the aroma dissipates, so it's best not to make more than you need.

KOMBU DASHI 

Combine 20 g (¾ oz) kombu with 600 ml (20 fl oz/ 2½ cups) water and leave to infuse overnight.
If you like, you can bring this to a very low simmer (do not boil the kombu) to extract a bit more flavour.

KATSUO DASHI

Combine 10 g (½ oz) kombu and 15–20 g (½–¾ oz) katsuobushi with 600 ml (20 fl oz/2½ cups) water and leave to infuse overnight. If you like, you can bring this to a very low simmer for a stronger flavour. Pass the finished dashi through a sieve (fine mesh strainer), pressing down firmly on the katsuobushi to extract as much of the liquid as possible.

MUSHROOM DASHI 

Combine 10 g (½ oz) kombu and 10–15 g (½ oz) dried mushrooms with 600 ml (20 fl oz/2½ cups) water. (Dried shiitake are preferable, but dried porcini are okay too – but I recommend using less of the latter, as their flavour is very strong.) Leave to infuse overnight. The mushrooms can also be boiled into the dashi to fully soften and extract a bit more flavour, but remove the kombu before doing this.

Dashigara Furikake
出汁がらふりかけ

SPENT DASHI FURIKAKE

MAKES ENOUGH FOR ABOUT 10 BOWLS OF RICE, PROBABLY MORE

One of the easiest things you can do with leftover dashi ingredients is make furikake. This also has the benefit of being shelf-stable – but you will get through it, especially if you use it in your cooking, not just as a rice seasoning. Check the recipes on page 27, 30 and 32 for inspiration.

INGREDIENTS

- rehydrated ingredients from making dashi (any type, page 23), drained and squeezed dry
- 2 tablespoons sesame seeds
- 1 tablespoon sugar
- 2 teaspoons MSG
- a little sesame or vegetable oil, for greasing
- 2 tablespoons flaky sea salt, lightly crushed
- aromatic seasonings, such as dried ginger, sanshō, shichimi, aonori, dried yuzu peel, etc., to taste

METHOD

Place the dashi ingredients in a food processor and blitz into small pieces. Stir this together with the sesame, sugar and MSG, then spread out in a thin, even layer on a baking tray (pan) oiled with a little sesame or vegetable oil.

Bake at 80°C (175°F/gas ¼) for 4 hours, stirring and redistributing the ingredients every hour or so, until completely dehydrated.

Leave to cool, then stir through the sea salt and any additional seasonings you like. Break up any clumps with your hands. Store in a jar in the cupboard for up to 3 months.

SPENT DASHI PUTTANESCA WITH SHICHIMI PANGRATATTO

SERVES 4

This is the first of several recipes in this book that might rankle Italians. Sorry, Italians! But also, don't worry! Your food culture is ancient and treasured and will easily withstand me messing around with it.

What you have here is actually a two-for-one recipe, because the shichimi pangratatto is really delicious and can go on all sorts of things. For me, the best thing about this recipe is how the kombu and katsuobushi integrate so well with the flavours of puttanesca, especially the savoury fishiness of the anchovies.

INGREDIENTS

- rehydrated ingredients from making Katsuo Dashi (page 23), drained and squeezed dry
- 4 tablespoons olive oil
- 25 g (1 oz) panko
- 1 teaspoon shichimi
- a few pinches of salt
- a few pinches of MSG
- 4 garlic cloves, smashed and thinly sliced
- 2–3 anchovy fillets
- 2 courgettes (zucchini), cut into chunky wedges
- 1 x 400 g (14 oz) tin finely chopped tomatoes
- 100 g (3½ oz) pitted olives
- 2 tablespoons capers
- ¼ teaspoon chilli (hot pepper) flakes, or more to taste
- 250 g (9 oz) spaghetti
- a few flat-leaf parsley or basil leaves, chopped

METHOD

Cut the rehydrated kombu from the dashi into very fine shreds, about 1–2 mm (1⁄16 in) thick and no more than 5 cm (2 in) long. Coarsely chop the katsuobushi. Heat 1 tablespoon of the olive oil in a frying pan over a medium heat, then stir in the panko, shichimi, salt and MSG. Cook, stirring frequently, until the panko is golden brown, then remove from heat and tip out into a bowl. Set aside.

Wipe out the pan, add the remaining olive oil and return to a high heat. Add the garlic, anchovies and courgettes and sauté for about 10 minutes, tossing frequently, until the courgettes have browned. Add the kombu and katsuobushi and continue to sauté for another 5–6 minutes, then add the tomatoes, olives, capers and chilli flakes. Reduce to a simmer and cook, covered with a lid, for about 15 minutes, stirring occasionally.

Cook the spaghetti according to the package instructions. Towards the end of cooking, add a ladleful of the pasta water to the sauce.

Drain the spaghetti well and toss through the sauce, keeping it on the heat as you do. Remove from the heat and stir through the parsley or basil. Divide among pasta bowls and garnish with the pangratatto.

SPENT DASHI FURIKAKE SALT & PEPPER CALAMARI ✯

SERVES 2

Incredibly, I never had salt and pepper squid until I moved to the UK at age 24. Twenty-four years without this delightful innovation of Cantonese-British cookery. In retrospect, it was a life hardly worth living, for what is there to live for other than the sensory thrill of crispy-chewy-salty-spicy squid? This version uses frozen breaded calamari – which, honest to God, turned out just as good if not better than any of the from-scratch versions I tested. This is what we call a 'massive win'.

INGREDIENTS

- 200–250 g (7–9 oz) frozen calamari
- 2 tablespoons oil
- 1–2 red chillies, sliced (use less if you don't want it too spicy)
- 2 garlic cloves, thinly sliced
- 2 cm (¾ in) chunk of fresh root ginger, peeled and thinly sliced
- 2 spring onions (scallions), chopped, white and green parts separated
- 2 tablespoons Spent Dashi Furikake (page 24), or similar fish- or seaweed-flavoured furikake
- ½ teaspoon shichimi
- ¼ teaspoon sanshō
- ¼ teaspoon white pepper
- a handful of coriander (cilantro), roughly chopped

METHOD

Cook the frozen calamari according to the package instructions – I always crank the heat up by about 10°C (20°F) more than what it says, to get it extra crispy. When the calamari is cooked, remove from the oven and set aside.

Heat the oil in a wok or large frying pan over a high heat. When it is shimmering hot, add the chillies, garlic, ginger and the white parts of the spring onions. Stir-fry quickly for 1–2 minutes until the garlic begins to brown, then add the calamari, furikake and spices. Stir-fry for another 1–2 minutes, tossing well to distribute the seasonings.

Remove from the heat, add the coriander and the green parts of the spring onions and toss well. Serve piping hot. It is excellent with beer.

Ninjin to Konbu no Sarada
人参と昆布のサラダ

CARROT & KOMBU SALAD

SERVES UP TO 4

This is a take on *carrotes râpées*, but with kombu and a Japanese dressing for a *wafū* twist. Similar dishes abound in Japan, and you can dress this however you wish – any of the dressings on pages 191–194 will work, or you can simply stir through a little sesame oil, vinegar and soy sauce. If you haven't got kombu, wakame or hijiki work, too.

INGREDIENTS

- 10 g (½ oz) kombu
- 3 large (or 2 very large) carrots
- 4 tablespoons salad dressing (Sour Plum and Shiso Dressing, page 194, is my preference, but any will work)
- 2 tablespoons sesame seeds

METHOD

Cover the kombu with water in a saucepan and set over a medium heat. Bring to a bare simmer, then switch off the heat and leave to cool completely. (Alternatively, you can make a dashi, as per the recipes on page 23, and retrieve the kombu at the end.)

Remove the kombu (keep the cooled dashi to use in another recipe), then cut it into thick ribbons about 5 cm (2 in) wide, then cut across the ribbons into very fine shreds.

Grate or finely julienne the carrots, and toss with the kombu, salad dressing and sesame seeds.

FURIKAKE-CURED SALMON

SERVES 4, AT LEAST

This salty-sweet salmon can be made from Spent Dashi Furikake (page 24) or any other kind you like. I like a mix of seaweed-based furikake and Yukari (a brand of shiso-flavoured furikake). Enjoy however you'd usually eat cured or smoked salmon, or simply have it grilled (broiled) and eaten on rice. It's also delicious on Furikake Focaccia (page 32) with cream cheese and chopped shallots.

INGREDIENTS

- 500 g (1 lb 2 oz) skinless and boneless salmon (or trout)
- 50 g (1¾ oz/3½ tablespoons) salt
- 50 g (1¾ oz/¼ cup) sugar
- 5 tablespoons furikake

METHOD

It is best practice to freeze any fish that is going to be served uncooked, especially if you are unsure of its freshness or provenance. Put the fish in the freezer overnight, then defrost it before proceeding with the recipe.

Stir together the salt, sugar and furikake until evenly mixed. Place half of this mixture in the bottom of a container that will fit the salmon, then lay the salmon on top of it. Pack the rest of the curing mixture on top of the salmon, then lay a piece of cling film (plastic wrap) over its surface. Put a lid on the container and refrigerate for 24 hours, turning the salmon over after about 12 hours to ensure an even cure. Do not leave the salmon in the cure longer than this, or it will become too firm and too salty.

To serve, brush off the curing solids and pat the salmon dry with paper towels. Slice the fish thinly, against the grain and at an angle, into wide strips.

FURIKAKE FOCACCIA ☆ ❦

SERVES 6, AT THE VERY LEAST

The base recipe for this super-simple bread comes from Helen Graves' wonderful *BBQ Days BBQ Nights*, a huge source of inspiration in my everyday home cooking. Helen describes focaccia as a 'confidence booster' because it's so easy to make, even for baking dum-dums like me. Hers is classically flavoured with a little rosemary; mine uses furikake instead for a subtle seaweedy Japanese note that works especially well with fish or soup.

INGREDIENTS

- 1 packet (7 g/¼ oz) instant yeast
- 1 teaspoon sugar
- 480 ml (16 fl oz/2 cups) lukewarm water
- 600 g (1 lb 5 oz/5 cups) plain (all-purpose) flour
- 5 tablespoons furikake
- 4 tablespoons sesame oil
- 1 tablespoon sesame seeds (black or white or a mix)
- 2 tablespoons vegetable oil, plus a little more for your hands
- a big pinch of sea salt (optional)

MAKE IT VEGAN

Use vegan furikake.

METHOD

Stir together the yeast, sugar and water in a large mixing bowl. Leave to sit for a few minutes to dissolve and activate the yeast. Add the flour, 3 tablespoons of the furikake, 2 tablespoons of the sesame oil and all of the sesame seeds and mix well. The dough will be very loose and sticky. Pour over another 1 tablespoon of sesame oil and and turn the dough over in the bowl to coat, with the aid of a spatula or dough scraper. Cover loosely with a lid or cling film (plastic wrap) and leave to prove for 2–4 hours until doubled in size.

Grease a large cast-iron skillet or baking tray (pan) with 1 tablespoon of the vegetable oil. Rub a little more oil on your hands and fold the sides of the dough over itself and into the centre four times, alternating the sides you fold each time (right to left and top to bottom). Tip the dough, fold-side down, into the skillet, and pour the remaining tablespoon of vegetable oil onto the surface of the dough. If you like things extra salty, sprinkle on some sea salt. Use your fingers to press deep divots into the dough all across its surface, then leave to rise again for another hour or so, until it's big and puffy and fills the pan.

Preheat the oven to 230°C (450°F/gas 8).

Bake for 30 minutes until well browned and cooked through, then brush the surface with the remaining tablespoon of sesame oil, and scatter over the remaining 2 tablespoons of furikake. Leave to cool briefly before slicing. This is ideally eaten straight away, but it will also last for a couple of days in an airtight container, and reheats well in a hot oven. It is an excellent vehicle for tinned or smoked fish.

味噌

CHAPTER 2

味
噌

MISO

You could do a whole book on MISO (味噌) – and people have! *The Book of Miso* (1976) by William Shurtleff and Akiko Aoyagi is the original and (probably) the best, with detailed information on its history and production, and a whopping 400 recipes, which is frankly just showing off. Shurtleff and Aoyagi were early adopters of Japanese fusion, with recipes like Miso Taco Sauce, Jambalaya with Miso and Banana, Peanut Butter and Sweet Miso Delight, preceding our current 'put miso in everything' trend by almost five decades.

There's just something about miso. People are mad for it. And who can blame them? It is at once salty, savoury, a little tangy and a little sweet, with a captivating aroma. Used sparingly, it seasons dishes and lends them a subtle complexity; used generously, it can make dishes punchy and intense. And it's all thanks to KŌJI (麹), the 'national fungus' of Japan, that's used to ferment it. Kōji contains a wealth of enzymes that break down protein into amino acids, to generate umami; starch into sugar, to create sweetness; and fat into volatile aroma compounds, to produce complex flavours. And all this comes from a pretty bland substrate of just beans and grains. Miso can become even more complex through extended ageing, which further breaks down its base ingredients through the Maillard reaction, resulting in deep flavours reminiscent of caramelised onions, kalamata olives and Marmite.

But what even is miso? A lot of people think it's a type of soup. And of course it *is* a soup, but it is so much more. Modern-day miso is derived from Chinese *jiang*, the broad category of fermented bean seasonings that also begat soy sauce and other Asian condiments, such as Korean *doenjang* and Thai *tao jiew*. While these seasonings have a lot in common in terms of their underlying production methods, their specific flavours vary enormously based on the cultures and ingredients used to ferment them. Miso is different from doenjang or tao jiew in the same way that Cheddar is different from Brie or Parmesan: so close, and yet so very far.

While kōji helps set miso apart from its continental counterparts, miso itself has a *very* broad range of flavours, and dozens of different types. Miso can be categorised by its ingredients, its regions, its fermentation methods, its texture and many other means, but for the vast majority of Japanese home cooking, you'll only need to understand four types:

WHITE (SHIRO / 白) MISO

Lighter-coloured miso, ranging from blonde to burnished brass, are miso that have not been aged for very long – typically just a few months. It usually has a lower concentration of salt but a little more sugar, and a lighter aroma with notes of fresh fruit, tangy cheese and fermenting dough (some white miso reminds me a lot of Belgian beer). In general, white miso is better for milder-flavoured foods, such as white fish and vegetables, but it's also a good go-to for a wide range of dishes. When I think of the flavour of miso, it's usually white miso I'm thinking of.

SWEET WHITE (SAIKYŌ / 西京) MISO/SWEET RICE MISO

Not to be confused with dengaku, also known as sweet miso sauce, sweet white miso is a very light miso associated with Kyoto. Traditionally, it is naturally sweet from using a high proportion of rice, which produces a lot of sugar during the fermentation process. Modern versions may add sugar, but either way, the result is a smooth, subtle, low-salt miso that retains the slightly nutty aroma of steamed rice and soy beans. It is a good choice for sweets.

RED (AKA / 赤) MISO

Red miso is miso that has aged for longer and has turned darker in colour, from amber on one end of the spectrum to mahogany on the other. Due to the loss of moisture by evaporation and prolonged enzymatic activity, red miso is more intensely savoury, with headier aromas of overripe or dried fruit, hard cheese and stout. The darker the miso, the stronger the flavour, so choose accordingly – save the really dark stuff for food that can match its intensity, like game, robust vegetables and mushrooms.

HATCHŌ (八丁) MISO

When I say 'the really dark stuff', this is what I mean. Hatchō miso is named for the Hatchō district of Okazaki where it's made, and it is distinguished by very extended ageing in cedar barrels – at least eighteen months, and sometimes over two years. This is an extremely dense miso, the colour of espresso, with a flavour to match: think molasses, dry-cured black olives, dates and cocoa. Because it's so dry and solid, it doesn't dissolve as readily into liquid as younger miso, so bear this in mind when mixing it into dishes. It will take more whisking to break up any lumps.

While we don't have anywhere near the range you'd find in Japan, there are many good brands of miso available these days. You can't go wrong with CLEARSPRING, who sell a variety of excellent (organic!) miso, including a sweet white and a Hatchō, and a few that are unpasteurised. HIKARI is a Japanese brand that does a good range as well. I particularly like their awase (mixed white and red) and nama-kōji (unpasteurised) miso.

If you're unsure about the quality of a particular brand of miso, check the label: ideally, it should contain only soy beans, rice (or other grains) and salt – sometimes with a bit of alcohol to act as a preservative. Some miso contains added dashi, which is great for making miso soup (its intended purpose), but not as good for general cooking. Any other additions are a red flag; miso should not contain aromatics like onions and chilli.

If you can find UNPASTEURISED (NAMA / 生 or NAMA KŌJI / 生麹) MISO), buy it! It tends to have a more complex (but sometimes slightly boozy) aroma, and it works better as a marinade because active kōji is a great tenderiser. Or if you can't find unpasteurised miso, you can have a go making it yourself. For that, I refer you to Kenji Morimoto's excellent *Ferment* (2025), which will teach you everything you need to know to get started.

MISOSTRONE WITH PANCETTA (HOMAGE TO FUMIO TANGA)

SERVES 4–6

Apologies to my friend Fumio Tanga, of the okonomiyaki pop-up Sho Foo Doh, who coined the term 'misostrone' many years ago. (Although a quick Google reveals that there have been others who couldn't resist this pun.) It is what it sounds like: minestrone seasoned with miso! Go for a white miso if you want to bring the tomatoes' sweetness and acidity to the fore, or use a dark red one to add a deep, rich savouriness.

INGREDIENTS

- 2 tablespoons olive oil
- 80 g (2¾ oz) pancetta lardons
- black pepper, to taste
- 1 onion, diced
- ½ bulb fennel, diced
- 1 large carrot, diced
- 4 garlic cloves, smashed and thinly sliced
- 1 teaspoon fennel seeds
- 1 teaspoon dried oregano
- 1 tablespoon tomato paste
- 1 x 400 g (14 oz) tin finely chopped tomatoes
- 5 g (¼ oz) kombu
- 1 bay leaf
- 1 x 400 g (14 oz) tin cannellini beans, drained
- 50 g (1¾ oz) small or broken pasta
- 60 g (2 oz/¼ cup) miso (any kind; see introduction)
- 50 g (1¾ oz) spinach (fresh or frozen)
- chilli (hot pepper) flakes, to taste (optional)

METHOD

Pour the oil into a large pot and set over a medium-high heat. Add the lardons and season with lots of black pepper, then sauté until well browned, about 8–10 minutes. Remove the lardons with a slotted spoon or fork and set them aside, then add the onion, fennel, carrot, garlic and fennel seeds to the pot. Stir well, cover and cook for about 10 minutes, stirring occasionally, until the onions are translucent and starting to brown in places.

Stir in the oregano and tomato paste and cook for another couple of minutes, then add the tomatoes, kombu and bay leaf. Fill the tomato tin twice with water and add to the pan too. Reduce the heat to medium-low and cook at a low boil, covered with a lid, for 20 minutes until the veg are soft.

Add the beans and pasta and continue to cook for another 10 minutes or so, until the pasta is done, stirring occasionally to ensure the pasta doesn't stick to the bottom of the pan.

Reduce the heat to low, remove the kombu and bay leaf, then whisk in the miso. You can do this by either holding the miso in a ladle and whisking it together with a little bit of broth before dispersing it through the soup, or by stirring it through a sieve (strainer) directly into the soup. Add the spinach and bring back to a high simmer so it wilts or thaws, then taste and add pepper or chilli flakes to taste.

Ladle the soup into deep bowls and garnish each one with a spoonful of lardons. Serve with crusty bread.

MAKE IT VEGAN

Simply omit the pancetta. If you want a similar salty-meaty topping, chopped olives are a good choice.

WEDGE SALAD WITH MISO RAMEN FLAVOURS ✯ ❦

SERVES UP TO 4 (ALTHOUGH IT'S THE KIND OF SALAD YOU COULD EAT AS A MAIN DISH, IN WHICH CASE IT WOULD SERVE 2)

Wedge salads are both ridiculous and sublime. Clearly, they are just a vehicle for eating bacon and ranch dressing. But the little devil on my shoulder asks: is this such a bad thing? This is a wafū version, drawing on the flavours of Sapporo miso ramen: garlic, ginger, sesame, salty pork and, of course, miso.

INGREDIENTS

- 10 g (½ oz/2 teaspoons) butter
- 80 g (2¾ oz) bacon, cut into lardons
- 3–4 garlic cloves, very thinly sliced
- 100 g (3½ oz) sweetcorn (ideally unsalted)
- 1 tablespoon white miso
- 20 g (¾ oz) pickled ginger (any kind), finely chopped
- 2 tablespoons rice vinegar
- 1 tablespoon mirin
- 3 tablespoons mayonnaise
- 20 g (¾ oz) menma (Japanese marinated bamboo shoots), chopped (optional)
- ½ head iceberg lettuce, cut into up to 4 wedges as desired
- about ½ bunch (10 g/½ oz) chives, finely sliced
- 2 big pinches of sesame seeds

METHOD

Melt the butter in a frying pan over a medium heat and add the lardons. Cook until they are well browned, stirring occasionally, then remove them from the pan with a fork or slotted spoon and set aside. Keep all of the rendered fat in the pan. Reduce the heat to low, then add the garlic and slowly fry until pale golden brown. Lift out and set aside as well. Add the corn to the pan and set over a very high heat. Stir-fry until the corn is browned, then remove from the heat and transfer the corn to the refrigerator in an open container to cool.

Stir the miso and pickled ginger into the fat in the pan while it's still warm, then tip it out into a bowl and leave to cool. When the miso-ginger mixture is no longer hot, stir in the vinegar, mirin, mayo and menma (if using). Pour the resulting dressing gluttonously over the iceberg wedges, then scatter over the lardons, fried garlic, corn, chives and sesame seeds.

MAKE IT VEGAN

Use plant butter and omit the bacon, but double the miso to pick up the saltiness.

THREE WAYS WITH MISO SOUP PACKETS

ALL RECIPES SERVE 4

I'm a big advocate of instant miso soup. There's just no easier way to complete a Japanese meal. Not all of them are good, of course, but some are excellent. If you buy the powdered kind instead of the kind that comes as a little sachet of paste, you've got yourself a dry miso seasoning that can be used in or on all sorts of things – popcorn, chips, fish, stir-fries, you name it. The following recipes are a few of my favourites.

MISO SOUP-SEASONED ROAST POTATOES 

If you've got a tried-and-true roast potato recipe, by all means use that. If not, here's mine: peel 1.5 kg (3 lb 5 oz) potatoes and cut them into chunky pieces – a good 3 cm (1¼ in) thick. Boil these in salted water for 12–15 minutes until fork-tender, but not falling apart. While the potatoes are cooking, heat 8 tablespoons neutral oil in a roasting tin in an oven set to 220°C (425°F/gas 7) for about 10 minutes.

When the potatoes are done, drain well, then trundle them around the pan with a lid on, so their edges become fluffy and floury. Tip the potatoes into the hot oil and toss them, so they are coated in oil on all sides. Roast for 30–40 minutes, turning the potatoes two or three times, until nicely browned all over.

Empty 2 packets (10 g/½ oz each) of powdered miso soup mix into a mortar and pestle and crush them, to break down any pieces of dried tofu or wakame. Transfer the potatoes to a mixing bowl, using a slotted spoon to leave behind any excess oil. Toss the potatoes with the miso soup mix and a big pinch of sesame seeds.

MISO SOUP-PACKET RISOTTO 

Melt 50 g (1¾ oz/3½ tablespoons) butter in a pressure cooker over medium-high heat. Add 1 finely chopped leek, 1 finely chopped celery stick, 200 g (7 oz) sliced mushrooms and 2 sliced garlic cloves. Sauté for about 3 minutes until the veg have softened slightly. Add 300 g (10½ oz) risotto or Japanese rice and cook for another 8–10 minutes, stirring often, to toast the rice. Add 6 tablespoons sake or white wine and let it boil for a few minutes to cook off the alcohol. Add 800 ml (27 fl oz/scant 3½ cups) stock, water or unseasoned dashi, then put the lid on the cooker and bring to full pressure. Cook for 8 minutes, then release the pressure and let the steam dissipate. When the cooker is depressurised, remove the lid and stir in 100 ml (3½ fl oz/scant ½ cup) single (light) cream and 2 packets (10 g/½ oz each) of miso soup mix. Taste and adjust the seasoning as you like with salt and pepper. This is delicious on its own and also vegan if you've used vegan miso soup and other plant-based ingredients, but it's also nice with fish.

ONE-PAN MISO SOUP-PACKET TUNA PASTA

Place 400 g (14 oz) short pasta (like fusilli or penne) in a saucepan with just enough water to cover. Bring to the boil and cook for as long as it takes for the pasta to soften and absorb most of the water; stir frequently. When the pasta is almost cooked through, stir in 120 ml (4 fl oz/½ cup) double (heavy) cream, 80 g (2¾ oz) cream cheese, 2 tins of tuna (drained), 180 g (6 oz) frozen peas and 4 packets (20 g/¾ oz) of miso soup mix. Let the pasta continue to boil until the sauce is thick and rich, then taste and add salt and pepper. You may also wish to add some capers and lemon zest, to balance the richness of the cream.

HIPSTER HISPI ☆ ❦

SERVES 2–4

If I were to open a modern British/sharing plates/natural wine/craft beer/farm-to-table/nose-to-tail/zero-waste/vegan/whatever restaurant in East London, this would be the first thing I'd put on the menu. Every restaurant like that needs a roasted hispi cabbage with stuff on it, and for good reason: it's so simple and so good. The addition of crisps as a garnish is stolen from a recipe Jay Rayner wrote, but I think he nicked the idea from someone else. Business as usual in the recipe-writing industry!

INGREDIENTS

- ½ hispi cabbage, outer leaves removed
- 2 tablespoons butter, at room temperature
- 2 tablespoons white miso
- 1 tablespoon chilli oil (ideally with bits)
- 1 tablespoon sesame seeds
- aonori flakes (or ½ sheet nori, cut or torn into tiny pieces), to garnish
- a handful of crisps (potato chips) (any flavour), crushed; some crispy fried onions; and/or Shichimi Pangrattato (page 25) – all optional, but all delicious, to garnish

METHOD

Preheat the oven to 220°C (425°F/gas 7).

Place the hispi into a small baking dish, cut side up. Smash the butter, miso and chilli oil into its surface, then sprinkle over the sesame seeds. Bake for 30 minutes until charred on the outside and just tender at the core, with varying degrees of softness in between.

Cut into chunks (scissors are helpful) and scatter over the aonori and crisps (or other bits) just before serving.

MAKE IT VEGAN

Use plant butter.

MISO FONDUE CHICKEN

SERVES 4

This dish is based on a baked chicken recipe my grandma used to make. Hers didn't have miso in it, but it's actually the perfect seasoning, matching the nutty flavour of the cheese and rescuing the chicken breasts from their own inherent blandness. Serve with steamed broccoli and any carb you like – rice, potatoes, bread, it's all good.

INGREDIENTS

- 120 ml (4 fl oz/½ cup) double (heavy) cream
- 30 g (1 oz/2 tablespoons) white miso
- 2 tablespoons white wine
- 1 garlic clove, grated
- 3 skinless chicken breasts (about 200 g/7 oz each), cut into thick chunks
- 50–60 g (1¾–2 oz) Swiss cheese, grated
- a handful of croutons (30–40 g/1–1½ oz)
- salt and pepper
- a handful of parsley or chives, finely chopped, to garnish

METHOD

Preheat the oven to 180°C (350°F/gas 4).

Whisk together the cream, miso, wine and garlic until no lumps of miso remain. Lightly season the chicken with salt and pepper, then transfer to a gratin dish and pour over the seasoned cream. Top with the cheese and croutons, then bake for 30 minutes, until the chicken is cooked through and the cheese is lightly browned.

Garnish with the parsley or chives before serving.

Nikumisuo no Arenji Mittsu
肉みそのアレンジ3つ

THREE WAYS WITH 'MAGIC MINCE'

MAKES 1 KG
(2 LB 4 OZ)
(SEE RECIPES FOR SERVING SIZES)

This is a recipe for nikumiso ('meat miso'), slightly rejigged from a recipe in *Your Home Izakaya*. My colleague Tim Hayward (the original and best Tim) once called this 'magic mince' because of its addictive deliciousness and versatility. Traditionally, you'd just have this on rice or noodles, but it has innumerable uses – hence the big batch size! Freeze some for later, in any of the suggested recipes below, or however you see fit.

INGREDIENTS

- 3 tablespoons oil (lard or dripping works well, too)
- 1 tablespoon sesame oil
- 2 onions, finely chopped
- 40 g (1½ oz) fresh root ginger, peeled and finely chopped
- 2 garlic cloves, finely chopped
- 1 kg (2 lb 4 oz) minced (ground) meat (any kind you like, but leaner mince is better)
- 100 g (3½ oz/scant 7 tablespoons) miso
- 4 tablespoons mirin
- 4 tablespoons sake
- 2 tablespoons soy sauce
- 2 tablespoons oyster sauce (optional)
- 2 tablespoons brown sugar
- 2 tablespoons sesame seeds (optional)
- 1 tablespoon Worcestershire sauce or tonkatsu sauce

Heat the oils in a frying pan over a medium heat. Add the onions and sauté for 8–10 minutes until softened and browned slightly. Add the ginger, garlic and mince, increase the heat to high and break up the mince into small crumbles. When the mince is cooked through, add the miso and stir through. Turn up the heat to high and keep cooking for about 5 minutes, so the meat and miso caramelise slightly, then add all of the remaining ingredients along with a splash of water. Cook for another 5 minutes or so, stirring frequently, until the liquid has evaporated and the meat is coated in a sticky glaze.

MAGIC MINCE 1: SLOPPY JOES

MAKES 6 PORTIONS

Dice 1 small carrot, 1 celery stick and 1 red (bell) pepper. Heat some vegetable or olive oil in a frying pan over a medium-high heat and add the veg. Sauté until softened, 8–10 minutes. Stir in 300 g (10½ oz) magic mince, 150 g (5½ oz) tinned beans or lentils and 400 ml (14 fl oz/generous 1½ cups) passata. Cook until the mixture is thick and jammy, stirring frequently. At the end, season to taste with any or all of the following: Worcestershire sauce, smoked paprika, barbecue sauce, ketchup, tonkatsu sauce, Tabasco, salt and pepper. To serve, scoop a big ladleful of the mixture into lightly toasted burger buns. It keeps for a few days in the refrigerator or a few months in the freezer, and reheats well in the microwave.

MAKE IT VEGAN

Soy mince or crumbled cotton tofu works great here. If you're using dehydrated soy mince, it will roughly triple in weight when rehydrated, so use about 330 g (11 oz) dried weight. The oyster sauce can be omitted or replaced with mushroom sauce. Use tonkatsu sauce (ensuring its vegan), instead of Worcestershire sauce.

MAGIC MINCE 2: SPICY SESAME NOODLES

MAKES 2 PORTIONS

Divide 3 tablespoons soy sauce, 2 tablespoons tahini, 2 tablespoons sesame seeds, 1–2 tablespoons chilli oil, 1 tablespoon rice vinegar, 2 teaspoons sugar and 2 teaspoons sesame oil between two noodle bowls. Stir the sauce well in each bowl, then cook and drain 2 portions of noodles – any kind you like, but ramen or udon work best. Rinse the noodles under running water, then drain and divide between the bowls. Mix well, then top with a big spoonful of magic mince (about 60 g/2 oz between the two bowls) and garnish with coriander (cilantro), julienned cucumber, sliced spring onions (scallions), bamboo shoots and plenty of chilli oil. (Alternatively, you can make these with the Garlic Miso Sesame Dressing on page 216.)

MAGIC MINCE 3: KEEMA CURRY

Simply add the magic mince to any prepared curry sauce you like – you will need about 100–120 g (3½–4 oz) magic mince per portion. Alternatively, you can make a simple dry curry: combine 100 g (3½ oz) magic mince with ½–1 tablespoon curry powder (depending on how strong/spicy you want it) and a glass of water in a pan. Set over a medium heat, bring to the boil and cook out the spices, stirring often, until the water evaporates completely. Scale up the quantities here to make as many portions as you need.

BONUS! MAGIC MINCE 4: HIYAYAKKO

See Four Ways with Chilled Silken Tofu, page 129.

WAFŪ RAREBIT ✯

SERVES 2

The combination of cheese and Japanese ingredients is no longer new to me, but I am still amazed by how well they go together. There are those that match, in terms of saltiness, aroma and even texture, like miso and nattō, and then there are those that contrast, like tonkatsu sauce and wasabi. Used in concert, they make an excellent rarebit – not one for the purists, but that leaves those of us who just want delicious cheesy toasty things.

INGREDIENTS

- 150 g (5½ oz) mature hard cheese, such as Red Leicester, Cheddar or Lancashire, grated
- 30 g (1 oz/2 tablespoons) unsalted butter, at room temperature
- 2 tablespoons tonkatsu sauce
- 2 tablespoons sake
- 1 tablespoon miso
- 2 teaspoons wasabi
- 2 chunky slices of bread, lightly toasted
- hot sauce and pickles, to serve (optional)

METHOD

Smash all of the ingredients, except the toast, together to form a rough paste, ensuring that the seasonings are well distributed among the cheese.

Spread the paste onto the toast and grill (broil) on the second-highest oven rack until gooey and browned (it needs a little while to fully melt and goo-ify the cheese, so don't rush this).

Leave to cool for just a few minutes before tucking in. Have hot sauce and pickles at the table (if you like), to cut through the richness as needed.

Matsukaze-yaki Fū Mītorōfu
松風焼き風ミートローフ

CHICKEN MEATLOAF, INSPIRED BY MATSUKAZE-YAKI ✭

SERVES 4

Inspiration comes in many forms. Often, it comes from Yuki Gomi, one of the UK's best Japanese cookery instructors and author of *Sushi at Home*. She recently posted a recipe for a dish called Matsukaze-yaki: minced (ground) chicken, seasoned with miso and mirin and other delightful things, which is then baked and often served as part of an osechi (New Year's) bento. I saw her video around the same time that I saw Antoni on *Queer Eye* make a meatloaf and I just thought ... damn, I need more meatloaf in my life. So here it is: a meatloaf that combines a few homey American elements with the flavours of Matzukaze-yaki.

INGREDIENTS

- 4–5 tablespoons boiling water
- 2 dried shiitake
- 1 onion, roughly chopped
- 2 garlic cloves, peeled
- 20 g (¾ oz) fresh root ginger, peeled and sliced against the grain
- 1 tablespoon sesame oil
- 1 tablespoon vegetable oil, plus extra for oiling
- 30 g (1 oz/2 tablespoons) miso (any kind)
- 2 tablespoons mirin
- 2 tablespoons soy sauce
- 1 tablespoon sugar
- 2 tablespoons panko
- 500 g (1 lb 2 oz) minced (ground) chicken
- 1 teaspoon aonori flakes, plus more to garnish
- 2 tablespoons cornflour (cornstarch) or potato starch
- 1 tablespoon ketchup
- 1 tablespoon Worcestershire sauce or tonkatsu sauce
- 2 tablespoons sesame seeds or white poppy seeds

METHOD

Pour the boiling water over the shiitake in a small dish and leave them to rehydrate for 15–20 minutes. Squeeze the shiitake dry and reserve the liquid. Cut the stems off the shiitake and discard, then combine with the onion, garlic and ginger in a food processor. Process until finely chopped. (Alternatively, this can be done by hand.)

Heat the oils in a frying pan over a medium-high heat. Tip in the onion mixture and sauté for 10–12 minutes, stirring frequently, until lightly browned. Add the reserved shiitake liquid and let it boil off. Remove from the heat and stir in the miso, mirin, soy sauce, sugar and panko. Ensure the seasoning is well mixed and there are no lumps of miso. Leave to cool.

Preheat the oven to 220°C (425°F/gas 7).

Tip the cooled mixture into a mixing bowl along with the chicken mince, aonori and cornflour. Mix everything well (best to use your hands for this), then transfer to a small (about 15 x 20 cm/6 x 8 in), lightly oiled loaf tin. Stir together the ketchup and Worcestershire sauce, and spoon or brush this over the top of the loaf. Scatter over the sesame or poppy seeds. Bake for about 30 minutes until a metal skewer inserted into the centre of the loaf comes out hot, or the internal temperature is at least 70°C (158°F).

Leave to rest for about 10 minutes before slicing and serving. This can also be served cold, sliced into squares or triangles and enjoyed in a bento. It's also nice dipped in ponzu.

Gyū hohoniku no akamiso shichū
牛ほほ肉の赤味噌シチュー

OX CHEEK STEW WITH RED MISO

SERVES 4

The flavour of this stew is incredibly rich and complex – it tastes like you've spent days making a classic demi-glace, but it only takes a few hours and uses just a handful of ingredients. Such is the awesome power of MISO!

INGREDIENTS

- a glug of olive oil
- 500 g (1 lb 2 oz) ox cheeks, cut into 4 big pieces
- 2 red onions, quartered
- 4 garlic cloves, peeled and smashed
- 30 g (1 oz/2 tablespoons) tomato paste
- 50 g (1¾ oz/generous 3 tablespoons) red miso (ideally Hatchō or brown rice miso, the darker the better)
- 250 ml (8 fl oz/1 cup) ruby port
- 250 g (9 oz) daikon, peeled
- 1 big carrot, peeled
- 20 g (¾ oz/1½ tablespoons) butter
- salt and pepper, to taste

METHOD

Preheat the oven to 120°C (250°F/gas ½).

Pour the oil into a medium casserole and set over a high heat. Add the ox cheeks and brown on all sides. Add the red onions and garlic and stir, then add the tomato paste and miso. When the onions and garlic have browned a bit, add the port and stir well to dissolve the miso and tomato paste. Top up with water to just cover everything, then add a baking paper cartouche and place a lid on the casserole. Transfer to the oven and cook for 4 hours.

Cut the daikon into rounds, about 2 cm (¾ in) thick, and the carrots into rounds, about 2.5 cm (1 in) thick. Remove the meat from the stew and set aside, then add the daikon to the pot and set over a medium-high heat. Boil the daikon with a lid on the pot, slightly ajar, for about 20 minutes until tender, then add the carrots and cook for a further 10–15 minutes until nice and soft. Stir frequently during this time and top up the liquid as needed to make sure it doesn't catch or over-reduce.

Add the meat back to the pot, then remove from the heat and stir through the butter. Taste and adjust the seasoning as you like with salt and pepper. Enjoy with rice, bread or potatoes.

MISO E PEPE

SERVES 2

Italy: once again, I'm sorry. This is cacio e pepe – pasta with cheese and pepper – but, you know, with miso. I can't help it if miso is such a versatile stand-in for cheese! It's pretty simple, but it requires some attention to get the sauce's consistency right. When you plate it up, it should look a little thin – this is because as it sits, the pasta will absorb water, and if too much water is absorbed, the emulsion will break and fat will separate out. It will still taste okay, but it will be oily rather than creamy, so keep that sauce loose!

INGREDIENTS

- 1 tablespoon olive oil
- 30 g (1 oz/2 tablespoons) butter
- 30 grinds of black pepper, plus a little more to finish
- 30 g (1 oz/2 tablespoons) white miso
- 150 g (5½ oz) spaghetti or linguine
- grated pecorino cheese, to garnish (optional)

METHOD

Heat the olive oil and butter together in a frying pan over a medium-high heat. Add the pepper and let it sizzle in the foaming butter for a few minutes, then whisk in the miso until no lumps remain.

Remove the pan from the heat and cook the pasta according to the package instructions.

In the final 1–2 minutes of cooking the pasta, add 2 ladlefuls of pasta water to the miso-butter mixture and raise the heat to bring it to the boil. If it's very watery, let it reduce in the pan for 1–2 minutes, but don't let it get too thick – the consistency should be more milky than creamy.

Drain the pasta and tip it into the pan, then quickly toss it through the sauce, switch off the heat and dish up. Garnish, if you like, with grated pecorino or some furikake.

MAKE IT VEGAN

Use plant butter, and vegan furikake to garnish.

TWO FLAVOURS OF NO-CHURN MISO ICE CREAM ✯

EACH RECIPE MAKES ABOUT 600 ML (20 FL OZ/2½ CUPS)

Malt and miso are gorgeous together and I've been making desserts with them for some time. This ice cream uses the old condensed-milk-and-whipped cream trick so it can set smoothly without an ice-cream maker, and the salt in the miso makes it a slightly softer scoop, too! I've also included a coconut version, a delicious vegan alternative. The coconut fat makes it quite rich, but a ripple of tart jam helps to balance it out.

INGREDIENTS

MALTED MISO

- 300 ml (10 fl oz/1¼ cups) double (heavy) cream
- 100 g (3½ oz/⅓ cup) condensed milk
- 50 g (1¾ oz/½ cup) Ovaltine
- 40 g (1½ oz/2½ tablespoons) smooth miso (white or red, but nothing too dark and definitely nothing lumpy)
- 1 teaspoon vanilla extract

COCONUT MISO BERRY SWIRL

- 250 ml (8 fl oz/1 cup) vegan whipping cream
- 200 g (7 oz/⅔ cup) condensed coconut milk (Biona is the brand I use)
- 30 g (1 oz/2 tablespoons) white miso or 40–50 g (1½–1¾ oz/2½–generous 3 tablespoons) sweet white miso
- 1 teaspoon vanilla extract
- a few spoonfuls of tart berry jam or compote

METHOD

For both recipes, combine everything (except the jam) in a large mixing bowl and beat with an electric whisk until thick and airy, similar in texture to Greek yoghurt (be careful not to overbeat, or the cream may split). Note that neither mixture will form peaks when fully whipped, and the coconut version will still be quite fluid – the main thing is that they should double in volume.

Once the mixtures are fully aerated, transfer to a container and cover. Freeze for several hours until completely set. When the coconut mixture has been in the freezer for about 1 hour and is semi-frozen, swirl the jam through it, then return it to the freezer to set completely.

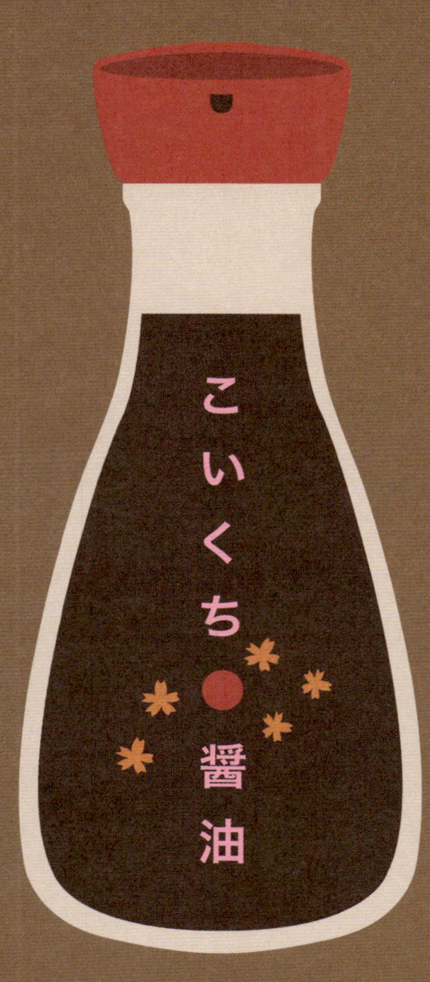
こいくち
醤油

CHAPTER 3

醤
油

SOY SAUCE

From the 4th century onwards, Japanese society was increasingly shaped by ideas and material culture from China, which included kanji, Buddhism and, of course, SHŌYU.

Although similar seasonings indigenous to the Japanese archipelago existed before the age of Chinese influence, like miso, Japanese soy sauce as we know it has roots in China's jiang traditions (page 36). Jiang became *shō* (醤) in Japanese, which then became shōyu (醤油) with the addition of the character for oil (or similarly viscous liquids). Shōyu was pronounced 'soi' in the Satsuma dialect, which is how it was first encountered by Europeans (the Dutch, to be precise), which became soy in English. Hence: soy beans are actually named after the sauce, not the other way around.

I am sure soy sauce is familiar to you, as it was familiar to me well before I began studying Japanese food. Kikkoman opened a soy sauce factory in Wisconsin in the 1970s, in response to growing North American demand. The factory was a huge driver of employment in central Wisconsin, so we've been proud Kikkoman people since before I was born. We always had it at home, and it wound up in a lot of our cooking when I was growing up.

Even if you are no stranger to soy sauce, it's worth discussing some of its finer points so you can live your best soy sauce life. First and most importantly: **Japanese soy sauce is different from Chinese soy sauce, and they are not interchangeable.** Production methods, base ingredients, fermentation cultures, etc. are very different in each country, so the finished products are very different, too.

One of the major differences between Japanese and Chinese soy sauces is that the 'light' and 'dark' distinction in Chinese soy sauces doesn't map to Japanese soy sauce. The distinction does exist, but the flavours are completely different; in fact, Chinese light soy sauce is closer in flavour to what might technically be called a dark soy sauce in Japan. It's confusing! So it's best to get 'light' and 'dark' out of your head completely, and instead learn the three most common categories of Japanese soy sauce:

ALL-PURPOSE SOY SAUCE, OR SIMPLY SHŌYU (醤油), OR KOIKUCHI (濃口)

This is your standard, go-to soy sauce that will be used in the overwhelming majority of Japanese home-cooked recipes. 'Koikuchi' technically means 'dark' or 'thick', but the flavour and colour are both far lighter than a Chinese dark soy sauce, which is why I avoid this translation entirely. All-purpose soy sauce is, as the name suggests, a good choice for just about everything – not too rich, not too light, with a strong but not overwhelming salinity. When I think of Japanese soy sauce, it is this flavour I think of.

TAMARI (溜り)

This is a richer, more viscous and darker variety of soy sauce, used where bolder flavours are required. Historically, tamari was a by-product of making miso – tamari is derived from the verb *tamaru* (溜まる), to accumulate, and it was the dark, delicious liquid that pooled at the top of miso as it aged. Modern tamari is more typically brewed as an ordinary soy sauce, but with a much higher proportion of soy beans and little or no wheat.

USUKUCHI (薄口)

Literally 'light' or 'thin' soy sauce, this is made with a higher proportion of wheat and water, resulting in a soy sauce with a much lighter colour and flavour, but more salt. This makes it excellent for seasoning dishes where you don't want a strong soy sauce flavour, or you want to preserve the colour of ingredients or clarity of broths.

The colours and flavours of Japanese soy sauces are derived from the ratios of wheat, soy beans and water used in production, as well as their age. When you buy Japanese soy sauce, it shouldn't contain sugar, colouring or any other additives – these are huge red flags in terms of quality, although there are some obscure regional styles of soy sauce that do add sugar. Typically, the only additive that should be used is alcohol, which acts as a preservative.

For specific brands, it's really very hard to go wrong with good old KIKKOMAN (another fun fact: the iconic Kikkoman bottle was designed by one of the original shinkansen designers, which is why it's so aerodynamic). Kikkoman does an unpasteurised soy sauce that I particularly love, though I do not really rate their tamari, which I find a bit lacking. Instead, I'd recommend CLEARSPRING again, whose tamari is strong yet smooth, widely available and not too expensive. In the US, look out for SAN-J, which specialises in premium tamari but also makes a shōyu and a range of table seasonings. For usukuchi, my go-to is HIGASHIMARU *marudaizu* ('whole bean'), which is spectacular in a bowl of chicken ramen. Lately I've also been loving a dashi shōyu (infused soy sauce) from ICHIBIKI, which is subtly flavoured with kombu and dried shiitake.

If you're looking to explore the outer limits of the ever-expanding shōyuniverse, have a browse on THE WASABI COMPANY's online shop, which features extensively aged shōyu, smoked shōyu, citrus-infused shōyu and many more varieties – all of them excellent. But as much as I love a new and novel soy sauce, I always come home to Kikkoman in the end. Maybe that's the Wisconsinite in me.

Hotate Bēkon Kushiyaki
帆立ベーコン串焼き

SCALLOP & BACON 'RUMAKI'

SERVES 2–4
(MAKES 6–7
SKEWERS, OR ABOUT
20 INDIVIDUALLY
TOOTHPICKED BITES)

Rumaki (bacon-wrapped vegetables, chicken livers or scallops on sticks) are irresistibly delicious; a crowd-pleaser. In terms of social cohesion, they have the potential to be a force for good. On the other hand, rumaki are a pseudo-Asian food item invented by Don the Beachcomber, emblematic of tiki bar Orientalism – a predecessor of the late 20th century Puck school of fusion (page 9). Rumaki's etymology is unknown, but it probably borrows 'maki' from Japanese, even though it isn't Japanese in origin. In fact, it has no real orgin, other than the Pacific Rim adventureland of Don the Beachcomber's mind. That said, there are very similar dishes commonly served throughout Japan at izakaya and kushiyaki joints. It's entirely possible these dishes are actually related, but who knows? Don the Beachcomber is long dead, so we cannot ask him.

INGREDIENTS

- 1 garlic clove, smashed and sliced
- 2 tablespoons soy sauce
- 2 tablespoons mirin
- 2 tablespoons port
- 1 tablespoon honey
- a few dashes of Worcestershire sauce (optional)
- many grinds of black pepper
- 200 g (7 oz) little scallops (about 20 in total)
- 10 rashers streaky bacon

METHOD

Stir together the garlic and all of the seasonings until well mixed. Use this to marinate the scallops for at least 1 hour, or overnight.

Preheat the grill (broiler) to high.

Cut the bacon rashers in half, then wrap each scallop in a piece of bacon, securing with toothpicks or bamboo skewers as you go. Grill (broil) for about 8 minutes, turning frequently, until the bacon is well browned and the scallops are cooked through.

BROWN SUGAR, BACON & SOY SAUCE ROASTED ROOT VEG

SERVES 4

This recipe could not be simpler and it could not be more delicious. (Go ahead and try – if you can make it more delicious, please email me so I can amend the recipe in future editions! You will be credited. But I still keep the royalties.)

INGREDIENTS

- 800 g (1 lb 12 oz) root veg or similar robust vegetables (radishes, cauliflower, carrot, parsnips, swede/rutabaga, sweet potatoes, etc. are all good)
- a glug of vegetable or olive oil
- 4 rashers streaky bacon
- black pepper, to taste
- a pinch of dried thyme (optional)
- 2 tablespoons soy sauce
- 2 tablespoons brown sugar
- 2 tablespoons mirin

METHOD

Preheat the oven to 200°C (400°F/gas 6).

Prepare the veg by peeling any that need peeling and cutting them into big chunks – a bit larger than bite-size. Pour some oil into something that can go from the stovetop to the oven, like a cast-iron pan or shallow casserole, and lay the bacon into it. Set over a medium heat and cook the bacon until crisp and brown, turning it often to ensure even cooking. Remove the bacon from the pan and set aside, then tip in the veg along with the pepper and thyme (if using) and stir them through the fat.

Transfer to the oven and roast for 35–40 minutes, tossing the veg a few times while cooking, until tender and well-browned.

Return the pan to the stovetop and set over a high heat. Stir in the soy sauce, brown sugar and mirin. Cook for a few minutes, stirring often, until the liquid reduces to a syrupy glaze. Remove from the heat, chop up the bacon, and stir it through the veg.

MAKE IT VEGAN

Simply omit the bacon; add a pinch of smoked paprika and some sea salt at the end to pick up the flavour.

SPICED & SEEDED TREACLE TAMARI RIBS ✯

SERVES 1–4

Oh my, these ribs are good. I ate two whole racks in about 15 minutes when I tested them. I'm not proud of this, but the appetite doesn't lie. This one's a winner.

INGREDIENTS

- 2 racks pork ribs (500–600 g/ 1 lb 2 oz–1 lb 5 oz each)
- 2 teaspoons smoked paprika
- 1 teaspoon cornflour (cornstarch)
- 1 teaspoon chilli (hot pepper) flakes
- 1 teaspoon curry powder
- 1 teaspoon fennel seeds
- salt and black pepper
- 1 batch Two-Ingredient Teriyaki (it's just 6 tablespoons tamari plus 4 tablespoons treacle/molasses, but a more detailed recipe is on page 210)
- 1 tablespoon pumpkin seeds
- 1 tablespoon sesame seeds
- 1 tablespoon sunflower seeds

METHOD

Preheat the oven to 150°C (300°F/gas 2).

Rub the ribs with all of the other ingredients except the pumpkin, sesame and sunflower seeds to coat them evenly. Lay each rack on a length of baking paper. Pour over any of the remaining sauce and seeds, fold up the edges of the paper and crumple them shut to enclose the ribs. Don't worry about forming a tight seal – it's okay if some steam escapes, but make sure the bones don't puncture the paper, so the sauce doesn't leak out. Place on a baking tray and bake the ribs in the foil for 1½ hours.

After this time, unfold the paper (but keep the ribs on it) and crank the oven up to 230°C (450°F/gas 8). Bake for a further 8–10 minutes, turning the ribs over halfway through cooking, until the ribs develop a bit of char.

Enjoy with white rice.

Shinpuru na Pirikara Teriyaki Chikin
シンプルなピリ辛照り焼きチキン

SIMPLE-SPICY-STICKY TERIYAKI CHICKEN ✯

SERVES 3–4

I tried to make a dish called 'chicken in waffles'. Yes, its dumb, but I have my reasons. The idea came from an old episode of *Treme*, where the chef character Janette develops a chicken and rice flour waffle dish. I could never quite imagine how it would have tasted, but regardless, the idea stuck with me – I loved the idea of rice cooked in a waffle iron. So many crispy bits!

So I cooked some spicy teriyaki chicken and sandwiched it between two layers of steamed rice in a waffle iron. The result was actually kind of *too* crispy, like eating a big, hard rice cracker. It was also a pain in the ass to get the rice out of the waffle iron. But luckily, it wasn't a total waste of time, because the chicken I made to put in the waffles was *delicious* – so here it is, minus the waffles. This is why we test recipes, folks!

INGREDIENTS

- 500 g (1 lb 2 oz) chicken thigh fillets
- 1 garlic clove, finely grated
- about 1 cm (½ in) chunk of fresh rot ginger, finely grated (no need to peel)
- 4 tablespoons soy sauce
- 2 tablespoons maple syrup, mirin or honey
- 1 tablespoon sesame oil
- 1 tablespoon ketchup
- ½–1 teaspoon shichimi (depending on how spicy you like it), plus more to garnish
- 1 tablespoon vegetable oil
- sesame seeds, to garnish

METHOD

Combine everything, except the sesame seeds, in a non-stick frying pan. Mix well to ensure the seasonings are evenly distributed and the chicken is well coated. Set over a medium-low heat with a lid on the pan and cook for 10 minutes, then turn the chicken over and cook for another 10 minutes, turning the chicken through the sauce a few times as it cooks. If there is any liquid left in the pan, turn the heat up and cook until nothing but a sticky glaze remains, turning the chicken frequently. If you are so bold, you can let the chicken blacken a bit. The main thing is that it should be sticky, not saucy. When the glaze is completely reduced, remove from the heat, slice and serve with rice or noodles and steamed greens.

KIMURA
ラムネ
ビー玉

Tsukimi Teriyaki Bāgā
月見照り焼きバーガー

TERIYAKI EGG BURGER

SERVES 4

Yes – another teriyaki recipe. But it's just so tasty, and there are so many ways to make it (and use it). Here, it adorns a burger with a fried egg, inspired by offerings from McDonald's Japan and my preferred Japanese fast food chain, Mos Burger. The tamari-garlic sauce has many other uses, too – it works best with richer flavours, such as duck, venison and salmon.

INGREDIENTS

4 tablespoons tamari

2 tablespoons mirin

2 tablespoons sake

2 tablespoons dark brown sugar

2 tsp cornflour (cornstarch)

1 garlic clove, smashed

1 cm (½ in) chunk of fresh root ginger, finely grated

a pinch of chilli (hot pepper) flakes

500 g (1 lb 2 oz) minced (ground) beef (DO NOT use lean beef – it needs to be about 20% fat or more)

a little vegetable oil, as needed

4 very thin slices of onion

a knob of butter

4 eggs

salt, pepper and MSG

4 burger buns

METHOD

Combine the tamari, mirin, sake, sugar and cornflour in a microwave-safe bowl and whisk until no lumps of cornflour remain, then stir in the garlic, ginger and chilli flakes. Microwave, uncovered, for 2 minutes, stirring the sauce every 30 seconds, until it's thick and glossy.

To cook the burger, you'll need either two big frying pans, or a griddle and a frying pan. The frying pan needs to be non-stick, to cook the eggs. Form the beef into four patties and lightly oil your griddle or pan. Press a slice of onion into the surface of each patty, and season the patties with pepper and a small pinch of salt. Heat the burger griddle or pan over a high heat, and set the egg pan over a medium heat. Add the butter to the egg pan and let it melt.

Once the griddle or pan is smoking, smash the patties onto its surface with a spatula. Crack the eggs into the melted butter in the other pan, and season them with a little salt, pepper and MSG. Cook the burgers for about 2–3 minutes, then flip them over. Flip over the eggs as well, then immediately turn off the heat under the egg pan. When the burgers have been turned, spoon the teriyaki sauce over each one, spreading it out with the back of the spoon to coat each patty evenly. After another couple of minutes, remove the burgers from the griddle and set into the buns. Top each patty with a fried egg. The yolks should be loose, but not completely liquid; if you're unsure about your egg-frying skills, you can cook them first and set them aside before frying the burgers, which are more forgiving.

Enjoy with fries or potato salad.

Tamago Kake Pasuta
卵かけパスタ

TAMAGO KAKE PASTA ✯

SERVES 1
(SCALE UP AS NEEDED)

This is a pasta-fied version of the perennial breakfast favourite, tamago kake gohan: rice with raw egg and soy sauce. And that's basically all this pasta is – think of it as a wafū carbonara, if you like. I just think of it as a delicious start to the day.

INGREDIENTS

- 1 egg
- a little sesame oil or olive oil
- a knob of butter
- 1–1½ tablespoons soy sauce or Mentsuyu (Noodle Soup Broth Concentrate, page 216)
- 100 g (3½ oz) spaghetti
- ½ sheet nori, snipped into fine shreds
- a pinch of shichimi (optional)

METHOD

Separate the egg and place the yolk in a little dish which has been oiled with a little sesame or olive oil. Place the white in a bowl with the butter and soy sauce or tsuyu and beat it together (it does not matter if the butter isn't melted, this is just to break it up a bit).

Cook the pasta as you like it, then drain it, let it cool for just a moment, then tip it into the egg white mixture and mix quickly to melt the butter and coat the noodles.

Transfer to a plate, then nestle the egg yolk in the middle and sprinkle the nori shreds and shichimi on top.

SOY SAUCE & SHICHIMI GUINNESS CAKE

SERVES 8–12

I have always thought that soy sauce and stout taste oddly similar, and I suppose this makes sense. Both products put grains or legumes through complex processes of cooking and fermentation, resulting in deep, rich, umami flavours. Which makes delicious cake, of course! The shichimi here adds a pokey heat, as well as subtle but amenable flavours of nori, sesame, orange and ginger.

INGREDIENTS

FOR THE CAKE

- 150 ml (5 fl oz/scant ⅔ cup) vegetable oil, plus a little more for greasing
- 240 ml (8 fl oz/scant 1 cup) Guinness (the export kind is better than Guinness draught)
- 180 g (6 oz/¾ cup) Greek yoghurt
- 1 tablespoon rice vinegar
- 200 g (7 oz/generous 1 cup) light brown sugar
- 100 g (3½ oz/generous ¼ cup) treacle (molasses)
- 2 tablespoons soy sauce
- 300 g (10½ oz/2½ cups) plain (all-purpose) flour
- 80 g (2¾ oz/⅔ cup) cocoa powder
- 1 teaspoon shichimi (optional)
- 1 teaspoon ground ginger
- 2 teaspoons baking powder
- 1 teaspoon bicarbonate of soda (baking soda)

FOR THE FROSTING

- 200 g (7 oz) white chocolate
- 200 g (7 oz/scant 1 cup) butter, softened
- 200 g (7 oz/scant 1 cup) cream cheese
- 350 g (12 oz/2¾ cups) icing (powdered) sugar
- 3 tablespoons soy sauce
- a pinch or two of shichimi

MAKE IT VEGAN

Plant-based yoghurt, white chocolate, butter and cream cheese will all work!

METHOD

Preheat the oven to 180°C (350°F/gas 4). Line the bases of two 23 cm (9 in) cake tins with baking paper and lightly grease them with a little oil.

In a large mixing bowl, whisk together the oil, Guinness, yoghurt, vinegar, brown sugar, treacle and soy sauce until well mixed. Whisk in all of the remaining ingredients for the cake batter, using a spatula to scrape down the sides of the bowl a few times. The batter should be fairly smooth, but some little lumps are okay.

Divide the batter between the prepared tins and bake for 30 minutes, or until a toothpick inserted into the middle of the cakes comes out clean. Leave to cool completely before frosting.

Melt the white chocolate in the microwave or a double-boiler, then set aside to cool for about 5 minutes – it needs to be melted and slightly warm, but not hot. Beat the butter and cream cheese together using an electric whisk, then beat in the icing sugar, soy sauce and melted white chocolate. Continue to beat until smooth and light.

Divide the frosting between the two cake layers, smoothing it out with a spatula or palette knife, then stack the layers up and decorate with a sprinkling of shichimi.

NO-CHURN SOY SAUCE CARAMEL ICE CREAM ✯

MAKES ABOUT 600 ML (20 FL OZ/2½ CUPS)

I whipped this up (literally) when I was looking to use up half a can of dulce de leche and some expired whipping cream. I have never rushed to write down a recipe so quickly. It's DELICIOUS.

INGREDIENTS

- 300 ml (10 fl oz/1¼ cups) whipping cream
- 200 g (7 oz/half a tin) dulce de leche (milk caramel)
- 2 tablespoons icing (powdered) sugar
- 1 tablespoon vanilla bean paste
- 1–2 tablespoons soy sauce (to taste)

METHOD

Combine everything in a large mixing bowl and use an electric whisk to whip the mixture until it is thick and airy, and holds soft peaks. Note: start with a little soy sauce and taste halfway through whipping, then add a little more if you want it saltier. Transfer to a container and freeze until set.

料理酒
本みりん
お
酢

CHAPTER 4

料理酒・味醂・米酢

SAKE, MIRIN & RICE VINEGAR

I often think of these three kōji cousins as the unsung heroes of Japanese cuisine, bringing balance to the forces of miso and soy sauce. Sake adds umami, a touch of sweetness, a little acidity and an unmistakable fermented rice fragrance. Mirin rounds out strong, salty flavours with a smooth, sherry-like sweetness. And rice vinegar brings mouthwatering sourness and its own fermented twang to the party.

I called them cousins, but actually they're more like a parent, a child and an uncle. Alright maybe this familial metaphor is a stupid way to explain it, but basically: mirin is a type of sake, and rice vinegar is a derivative of sake. Sake, of course, is rice liquor, fermented (not distilled!) from rice, saccharified by our old friend kōji. The resulting booze is a little stronger than wine (normally around 16–18%) and full of amino acids, which we perceive as savoury and rich flavours. It usually has a bit of residual sugar as well, and sometimes a touch of lactic acid. I sometimes describe sake as like liquid sourdough bread for this reason (and indeed, some old-school styles of sake are spontaneously fermented using airborne local microbes in a similar way).

Sake is called NIHONSHU (日本酒), 'Japanese alcohol', in Japan, but the kind you'll be cooking with is called RYŌRISHU (料理酒), or 'cooking alcohol'. This is a low-grade sake with added alcohol as a preservative, and added salt to prevent people from drinking it, thereby avoiding alcoholic beverage taxes. As a drink, it's pretty rough (although you can actually use it in cocktails, see page 91) – but that's not what it's for. It's for providing an earthy umami base upon which to build bolder flavours. The alcohol in sake also has its own unique effects, boosting some aromas while reducing others (especially fishy and meaty smells), and tenderising proteins while strengthening pectin, helping vegetables hold their shape during cooking.

These effects are also contributed by MIRIN (味醂), a unique sub-category of sake in which fermentation is halted before it is complete by adding a large amount of distilled alcohol, killing the remaining yeast and leaving behind a high quantity of unfermented sugar. Mirin made this way is called HON-MIRIN (本みりん), 'true mirin', and it has much of the same umami and fragrance as sake, but with a strong sweetness that sits somewhere between honey and Amontillado sherry. Unlike cooking sake, hon-mirin doesn't have added salt, which makes it susceptible to double duty: taxed as an alcoholic drink both in Japan and again when it's imported. Accordingly, hon-mirin is expensive. Enter MIRIN-STYLE SEASONING (mirin-fū chōmiryō / 味醂風調味料). This is a cheap, mirin-like product designed to avoid alcohol taxes and work in place of real mirin.

But does it? In the past, my position was yes, absolutely. It is mostly there to add sweetness, I figured, so it didn't matter if you're not getting much in terms of aroma or alcohol from it. And besides, this is what would be used in the majority of cooking in Japan, so it's perfectly legitimate in that sense. But recently, I have reconsidered this opinion and decided that no, YOU REALLY SHOULD BUY HON-MIRIN, because you *are* looking for more than just light sweetness from it. Mirin should contribute its own aroma, umami and character to dishes. So I say: splurge on a bottle of decent hon-mirin, because it will make a noticeable difference in your cooking. Once again, CLEARSPRING does an excellent one, their bold, nutty Mikawa mirin. But my go-to hon-mirin is HINODE, which is very affordable and not too strong – some hon-mirin can actually be a little overpowering, but Hinode has a softer aroma that works well in pretty much everything.

Having said that, mirin-style seasoning is often a better choice for dishes where the mirin will be overwhelmed by stronger flavours, such as tamari or anything spicy. In these cases, hon-mirin would be wasted. (And on a similar note: don't use expensive drinking sake for cooking!)

RICE VINEGAR (KOMEZU / 米酢, or just SU / 酢) is another sake-adjacent product, originally made by re-fermenting sake using a vinegar culture. However, as this method is expensive, modern Japanese vinegars are now more commonly made from a mixture of rice and other grains, or sake lees. Japanese vinegar has a relatively low acetic acid content, which makes it mellow and versatile in cooking. There are, of course, many varieties of premium Japanese vinegars, including ones that are aged in wood, or in ceramic vessels warmed by the sun, turning amber (AKAZU / 赤酢) or almost black (KUROZU / 黒酢) over time.

But don't worry about those – in most Japanese cooking, vinegar is there primarily to provide a bright, clean acidity that won't be too overpowering. For the recipes in this book, and indeed most Japanese recipes in general, any cheap Japanese rice or grain vinegar will be just fine. In terms of brands, you can't go wrong with MIZKAN, who have been in the vinegar business since the early 1800s.

Yūrin Nasu
油淋なす

CHINESE-JAPANESE FRIED AUBERGINE WITH TANGY LEEK SAUCE ☆ ❦

SERVES 2

This is a common vegetarian variation of the Chinese-Japanese dish *yūrinchī*: fried chicken, smothered in mouthwatering sauce made from chopped leeks, ginger and a generous glug of vinegar. This recipe uses pan-fried aubergine (eggplant) instead of deep-fried chicken, which is just as juicy, moreish and flavourful.

INGREDIENTS

- 1 big aubergine (eggplant), cut into long batons or wedges no more than 2 cm (¾ in) thick
- 1 tablespoon sake
- 3 tablespoons soy sauce
- 1 baby leek, finely diced
- 2 cm (¾ in) chunk of fresh root ginger, peeled and grated
- 1 garlic clove, grated
- 3 tablespoons rice vinegar
- 3 tablespoons light brown sugar
- 1½ tablespoons sesame oil
- 1 tablespoon mirin
- a pinch of chilli (hot pepper) flakes or shichimi (optional)
- vegetable oil, as needed for shallow-frying
- 6 tablespoons cornflour (cornstarch) or potato starch

METHOD

Toss the aubergine with the sake and 1 tablespoon of the soy sauce. In a separate bowl, combine the remaining soy sauce with the leek, ginger, garlic, vinegar, sugar, sesame oil, mirin and chilli (if using). Stir well, then microwave for 30 seconds–1 minute to warm it through and dissolve the sugar; the leek should still be raw, so don't let it get too hot. (You can also heat it until just steaming in a pan on the stovetop.)

Pour the vegetable oil into a large frying pan to a depth of about 5 mm (¼ in) and set over a medium-high heat. Toss the seasoned aubergine in the cornflour. When the oil is hot, lower the aubergine into the oil and fry for about 10 minutes, turning often, until browned all over. Remove the aubergine from the pan to drain on paper towels.

Transfer the aubergine to plates and pour over the leek sauce. Enjoy with plenty of white rice.

Chikin Tendā Nanban
チキンテンダー南蛮

CHICKEN TENDERS NANBAN ✯

SERVES 4

Nanban was the name of my restaurant and first cookbook; it means 'southern barbarian', and was originally used to describe Europeans, as they first arrived in Japan in the south, via Southeast Asia. I chose it as a recognition of my own status as a brash and idiotic outsider, but also to draw attention to the history of foreign influence in Japan's cuisines. Chicken Nanban is a dish from Miyazaki prefecture that bears several hallmarks of what was called 'nanban' cookery: vinegar, chilli, tartare sauce and deep-frying in batter. The dish requires two sauces – a sweet ginger vinegar and a chunky Japanese tartare sauce – so it's a bit prep-heavy, but you can make the whole thing easier by using store-bought chicken tenders. They work surprisingly well! (See also: in the Style of Scampi Katsudon, page 86.)

INGREDIENTS

- 3 tablespoons rice vinegar
- 2 tablespoons mirin
- 2 tablespoons soy sauce
- 2 tablespoons sugar
- 1 tablespoon lemon juice
- 1 teaspoon finely grated fresh root ginger
- a pinch of chilli powder or shichimi
- 4 portions chicken tenders, nuggets, or similar frozen/breaded chicken product
- 1 batch Japanese Tartare Sauce (page 200)
- rice and salad or shredded cabbage, to serve

METHOD

Combine all the seasonings in a saucepan or microwave-safe bowl and bring to the boil, either on the stovetop or in the microwave. Stir to ensure the sugar is dissolved, then leave to cool.

Cook the chicken according to the package instructions, perhaps for a couple minutes longer than specified, to help them get extra crispy.

Place the chicken on a plate along with some rice and salad or shredded cabbage. Spoon over the sweet ginger vinegar and serve with the tartare sauce on top.

宮崎日南塚田農場 直送直営之証

Sukanpi no Katsudon-Fū
スカンピのカツ丼風

SCAMPI IN THE STYLE OF KATSUDON ✯

SERVES 2

Katsudon is a rice bowl topped with tonkatsu that is lightly poached in a mixture of seasoned dashi, onions and eggs. Like many recipes involving tonkatsu, it also works well with fish fingers or scampi. Can we take a moment to appreciate scampi? Langoustine tails, conveniently breaded and ready to cook, right there in the freezer. What luxury! What a time to be alive!

INGREDIENTS

- 200–250 g (7–9 oz) scampi
- 2 baby leeks, thinly sliced at an angle
- 120 ml (4 fl oz/½ cup) dashi
- 3 tablespoons soy sauce
- 2 tablespoons mirin
- 2 tablespoons sake
- 50 g (1¾ oz) spinach (fresh or frozen whole leaf, defrosted)
- 3 eggs, loosely beaten
- 2 portions of cooked rice
- ¼ sheet nori, finely snipped with scissors, or aonori, to garnish
- shichimi, to taste (optional)

METHOD

Cook the scampi according to the package instructions, but give them a couple of extra minutes so they are extra crispy. Combine the leeks, dashi and seasonings in a small frying pan and bring to the boil. Cook for about 8 minutes until the leeks are nice and soft. If the scampi are done at this point, carry on with the recipe. If not, remove the pan from the heat and wait until they're done.

When the scampi are out of the oven, add the spinach to the pan and bring it back to the boil. Pour in the eggs and briefly stir them through the dashi. When the eggs are about halfway set, stir again, then place the scampi on top. Continue to cook for another 2–3 minutes, so the dashi soaks into the bottom of the scampi. (The eggs should still be loose on top.)

Divide the mixture onto two bowls of hot rice, and garnish with nori and shichimi (if you like).

Kani to Nori no Omuretsu
カニとのりのオムレツ

CRAB & NORI OMELETTE ✯

SERVES 1–2

This luxurious omelette was inspired by some I saw on Instagram at fancy London restaurants. I don't get out much, so I have to experience nice restaurants vicariously through social media and my own home cooking. Which is fine! My version is gloriously rich, with a good glug of mirin to underscore the natural sweetness of the crab.

INGREDIENTS

- a generous knob (30–40 g/1–1½ oz) butter
- ½ sheet nori, torn into little bits
- 2 tablespoons mirin
- 50 g (1¾ oz) picked crab meat (use white or a 50:50 mix of white and dark meat; all dark meat is too rich)
- 3 eggs
- salt, MSG and white pepper, as needed
- chives, finely chopped, to garnish

METHOD

Melt about half of the butter in a small, reliably non-stick frying pan over a low-medium heat, then tip in the nori. Gently sauté the nori for a minute, then add the mirin and cook for another few minutes to cook off the alcohol and fully soften the nori. Remove from the heat and stir in the crab. Tip this mixture into a dish and set aside, using a flexible spatula to scrape the pan clean.

Beat the eggs well with a generous pinch of salt and a little MSG and white pepper. Set the pan back onto a medium-high heat and add most of the rest of the butter (you'll need about ½ teaspoonful to finish the omelette). When the butter is foaming, tip in the eggs and rapidly scramble for just a minute or two, leaving them very runny on top but lightly set on the bottom. Tip the crab-nori mixture onto one side of the eggs, then reduce the heat to low and use a spatula to roll the eggs up around the crab, like a carpet. Remove from the heat, then melt the remaining butter over the top of the omelette and serve garnished with chives, with rice or toast.

Tataki Kyūri no Rāyu Ae
たたききゅうりのラー油和え

SMACKED CUCUMBERS WITH VINEGAR & CHILLI OIL

SERVES 2–4

I always seem to have a glut of chilli oil, because I make it myself, but also people are always gifting it to me. I must give off chilli oil vibes (which is correct – please keep gifting me chilli oil!). If you also have too much, this is a good way to use quite a lot of it – cucumbers have a natural cooling effect so you can enjoy the oil for more than just its heat.

INGREDIENTS

- 1 cucumber
- 4 tablespoons soy sauce
- 3 tablespoons rice vinegar
- 1 tablespoon sugar
- 1 tablespoon sesame seeds, crushed
- ½ garlic clove, finely grated
- 2 tablespoons chilli oil (page 197)

METHOD

Pound the cucumber with your fists or a rolling pin several times so it fractures into irregular chunks. Cut the cucumber into wedges using the rangiri technique: slice it at a 45-degree angle, rotating the cucumber a quarter turn with each cut. Dress the cucumber in all of the remaining ingredients, well mixed. Serve very cold.

COOKING SAKE SALTY DOG

SERVES 1

Cooking sake has salt and vinegar added to it so people can't drink it in great quantities, thereby avoiding duties on alcohol. But in some drinks, a bit of salt is desirable, so cooking sake actually works. It adds an interesting savouriness to Martinis, and it's also right at home in a Bloody Mary. Here, I've used it in a classic Salty Dog, taken into Paloma territory with a squeeze of lime and a splash of soda.

INGREDIENTS

- ice
- 2 shots (50 ml/1¾ fl oz/3½ tablespoons) cooking sake
- 75 ml (2½ fl oz/5 tablespoons) grapefruit juice
- juice of ¼ lime
- a splash of something sweet and fizzy (lemonade, orange soda, ginger ale, tonic, Ting, whatever)
- a slice of lime or grapefruit, to garnish

METHOD

Fill a tumbler with ice and add the sake, grapefruit juice and lime juice. Stir well, then top with the fizzy drink and garnish with the citrus slice.

HON-MIRIN OLD FASHIONED ✯ ❦

SERVES 1

Good mirin has a delicious sherry-like quality with notes of walnuts, dried fruit and caramel. This makes it excellent in cocktails, especially an Old Fashioned, where it can replace the standard sugar cube with a more sophisticated sweetness and a slight savouriness. This works with whiskey or brandy, but for Wisconsinites like me, brandy is the only choice.

INGREDIENTS

- 1 shot (25 ml/1 fl oz/1⅔ tablespoons) good-quality hon-mirin
- 2 shots (50 ml/1¾ fl oz/3½ tablespoons) brandy
- several dashes of bitters (Angostura or orange, or a mix of the two)
- a few ice cubes
- a strip of orange zest
- 1 cocktail cherry

METHOD

Combine the mirin, brandy and bitters in a tumbler and swirl the glass to combine. Add the ice and orange zest and stir very well. Garnish with the cherry.

Hon-Mirin no Mon Buran
本みりんのモンブラン

HON-MIRIN MONT BLANC ✭

SERVES 4

Mont Blancs are one of my all-time favourite desserts. I wish I had one right now. Oh wait, I do, because I just tested this recipe and it's awesome! The sherry-like aroma of hon-mirin is a perfect swap for the usual brandy or Armagnac – in fact, I prefer it, as it's less boozy and more smooth.

INGREDIENTS

- 350 g (12 oz) vacuum-packed chestnuts
- 4 digestive biscuits (graham crackers)
- 8 soft pitted prunes or dates
- 30 g (1 oz/¼ cup) plain (all-purpose) flour
- 50 g (1¾ oz/generous ¼ cup) light brown sugar
- 1 teaspoon baking powder
- ¼ teaspoon ground cinnamon
- salt, as needed
- 4 tablespoons milk
- 2 tablespoons vegetable oil, plus extra for greasing
- 1 teaspoon sesame oil
- 1 teaspoon rice vinegar
- 3 teaspoons vanilla bean paste or extract
- 70 g (2½ oz/scant ⅓ cup) caster (superfine) sugar
- 6 tablespoons hon-mirin
- 250 ml (8 fl oz/1 cup) whipping cream
- 4 tablespoons icing (powdered) sugar, plus extra for dusting
- 4 meringue nests

METHOD

Preheat the oven to 180°C (350°F/gas 4).

To make the chestnut cake, place 50 g (1¾ oz) of the chestnuts in a food processor with the digestives. Blitz to a fine crumb, then whizz in the prunes, followed by the flour, brown sugar, baking powder, cinnamon and a big pinch of salt. Add the milk, oils, vinegar and 1 teaspoon of the vanilla and blend until smooth.

Divide the batter among four lightly oiled cupcake tins and bake for 20 minutes. When they're done, leave to cool in the tins, then tip them out and cut the rough tops off each cake so you have four little cylinders.

To make the chestnut purée, combine the remaining chestnuts in a saucepan with the caster sugar and enough water to cover the chestnuts. Bring to the boil and cook until the liquid is a very thick, sticky syrup, stirring frequently, especially towards the end of cooking to ensure the chestnuts don't scorch. Remove from the heat, then retrieve four of the prettiest, plumpest chestnuts and set them aside for decoration. While still warm, blend the rest of the chestnuts and their syrup in a food processor along with the hon-mirin, 2 tablespoons of the cream, 1 teaspoon of the vanilla and a pinch of salt to a smooth purée. The purée should be very thick, but if it is so thick it won't blend, add a little water (1 tablespoon at a time) until it can be blended evenly. Chill the purée in the refrigerator.

Whip the remaining cream with the icing sugar and the remaining teaspoon of vanilla until it forms stiff peaks.

To assemble the Mont Blancs, place a dab of whipped cream in the well of each meringue nest, then lay a chestnut cake on top. Cover the whole thing in whipped cream (use a piping bag), then top with the chestnut purée. If you have a potato ricer (the tool of choice), place the purée inside the ricer and squeeze it out onto the top of each cake. If you don't have a ricer, you can pipe the chestnut purée on top, or just dollop it with a spoon. Decorate with the reserved candied chestnuts and a generous dusting of icing sugar.

CHAPTER 5

ご飯・麺類物

RICE & NOODLES

Rice and noodles are grouped together here because they usually occupy the same space in Japanese meals: the carb space. For the most part, you'll always have one or the other, which means you'll always want some on hand. RICE (GOHAN / ご飯 or MESHI / 飯 when it's cooked, KOME / 米 when it's uncooked) is a little more straightforward than NOODLES (MEN / 麺), so let's discuss that first.

For as long as there has been any semblance of a cohesive Japanese nation-state, there has been rice. Before this, some 3,000 years ago, the people of the Japanese archipelago subsisted on acorns and other foraged foods. Rice cultivation was initially concentrated in the hotter southwestern half of Japan, which supported an enormous, unprecedented population boom – from about 600,000 to over five million in about 800 years. This growth was almost entirely concentrated Kyushu, Shikoku and western Honshu, where rice was more easily grown.

Over time, rice came to completely dominate Japanese agriculture, and its significance in Japanese society deepened with its inclusion in religious and political systems: it was used as offerings to both deities and warlords. The importance of rice in Japanese cultural identity is hard to understate; the anthropologist (and fellow Wisconsinite!) Emiko Ohnuki-Tierney wrote a whole book about it, called *Rice as Self* (1993). So if you're going to cook Japanese food, you're going to cook rice. There's a reason why the word for cooked rice (gohan) is the same as the word for 'meal' – they are synonymous, in so many ways. Rice is there for nutrition, for balance, and for satisfaction. It's there because it has to be there.

I always advise buying rice from a Japanese or Asian supermarket, because you will find better quality and value there. The range of rice stocked by a specialist is little better across the board. YUMENISHIKI is a good brand that's now sold at many supermarkets, but currently my favourite Japanese rice is YUMEPIRIKA from Hokkaido. CLEARSPRING's rice is very good, too. Note that some Japanese rice is sold as 'sushi rice.' I avoid anything labelled as such out of principle (a principle I call 'being an insufferable pedant') because this isn't actually sushi rice. Sushi rice is rice that's been cooked and seasoned in a certain way (page 100) for making sushi, *not* a type of rice!

Premium brands aside, another thing to look out for when buying Japanese rice is packaging. It's better to buy rice that's been vacuum-packed into hard bricks, rather than rice that's packaged loose in a box or a floppy bag. This is because as the rice is transported, the grains rub against each other, creating a fine dust of rice flour that makes the rice gluey, and possibly even breaking the grains.

At various points in Japanese history, rice was not the most affordable carb. Market fluctuations and food fashions have driven demand for other grains, namely wheat and buckwheat, the raw ingredients for Japan's big three noodles: UDON (うどん), SOBA (そば) and RAMEN (ラーメン). All of these are derived from Chinese progenitors, but they appeared at different points along the noodle timeline. Some form of proto-udon dates back to the 8th century; soba noodles were first recorded in the Edo period, but related buckwheat soup dumplings appeared around the 13th century; and ramen arrived at the end of the 19th century. Each noodle has its own unique culture, craft, flavour and texture, so DO NOT SUBSTITUTE ONE FOR THE OTHER!

Soba are thin, brittle and grainy, with a distinctive nuttiness. Udon are chubby and soft, with a mochi-like chew. Ramen is the most variable, and can be thin and straight or thick and wavy and everything in between, but it must be made with wheat flour and additives called kansui, which give ramen its characteristic springy texture. A few things to look out for when shopping:

SOBA

Soba mainly varies in terms of its buckwheat-to-wheat ratio. I generally buy soba that's a minimum 80% buckwheat, but this is a personal preference, as I like a strong buckwheat flavour. Do not buy Korean buckwheat noodles – they have a completely different flavour and texture, which is much more starchy.

UDON

Most udon is sold in vac-packed ambient pouches, ready to eat after loosening them in hot water. These almost never have a strong chew, and are often very fragile, breaking apart even with fairly gentle cooking. Among this type of udon, ITSUKI is one of my favourite widely available brands, but in general I prefer frozen udon. YUTAKA is excellent – doughy and toothsome.

RAMEN

Decent plain ramen noodles are frustratingly hard to buy. This is partly because the best ramen is fresh, not dried, but it's also because 'ramen' has come to be used for pretty much any Asian noodle, when in actuality it is a very specific thing: wheat noodles made with kansui (potassium carbonate [E501] and/or sodium carbonate [E500]) to enhance the gluten structure of the dough. Check the label – no kansui, no ramen. Many Asian supermarkets in the UK stock refrigerated fresh ramen made by the manufacturer WINNER, which are probably the best ramen noodles you're likely to come across. Very few other brands hit the brief, which is why I usually fall back on good old instant ramen, which is made with kansui and therefore has the correct texture. My preferred brands of are NISSIN, MARUCHAN, and Samyang and Ottogi's 'plain' noodles from Korea.

One last thing about noodles: because of the overwhelming popularity of soba during the Edo period, 'soba' came to be a catch-all term for noodles – which is why the word is still used in some non-soba dishes, like yakisoba. This shouldn't use actual soba – a mistake I made early in my Japanese food journey, resulting in a lot of stir-fries with sad, broken noodles. Read the recipe, and use the right noodle for the job!

Gohan
ご飯

RICE

SERVES 4
(SCALE UP AS NEEDED – THE METHOD IS THE SAME)

Japanese cooking job one: learn to cook rice. So here it is, my tried-and-true method. Remember: use short-grain Japanese rice, trust the process, and all will be well.

INGREDIENTS

300 g (10½ oz/1⅓ cups) Japanese rice

400 ml (14 fl oz/generous 1½ cups) water

METHOD

Wash the rice in three or four changes of water, then drain well and place in a saucepan with the measured water. If you have time, leave it to soak for about 1 hour – this will result in a more even texture, but it is not necessary. Set the pan over a high heat and bring to the boil, then place a lid on the pan and reduce the heat to low. Set a timer for 15 minutes and don't remove the lid during this time. When the timer is up, switch off the heat and let the rice rest for 5–10 minutes, then serve.

VARIATION: ZAKKOKU (MULTIGRAIN) RICE

Simply replace up to half of the rice with other whole grains – you can use anything that cooks quickly, so bulgur, buckwheat, oats, millet and cracked freekeh are all good choices.

VARIATION: SUSHI RICE

To make sushi rice, cook as above, then tip the rice out into a wide bowl. Sprinkle over 5 tablespoons/half a batch of Sushi Vinegar (page 203) and use a rice paddle or spatula to cut the vinegar into the rice as it cools. This will make enough for about 30–32 pieces of sushi.

VIRAL RICE (WITH APOLOGIES TO EMILY MARIKO)

SERVES 4

A while back there was this viral video going around by an influencer named Emily Mariko, in which she calmly and quietly cooked a delicious-looking lunch made of leftover rice and salmon, topped with with Kewpie mayo, Sriracha sauce, kimchi and Korean nori. My wife sent me this video with a message along the lines of 'look, she's eating what you eat when you're drunk'. And yet somehow Emily Mariko made it look healthful and chic. This is, I suppose, why I have never made much headway as an influencer. I tend to make things look *less* healthful and chic, just by virtue of being a slovenly and perpetually tired-looking middle-aged man.

This is my take, which I have takikomi gohan-ified by cooking everything together in one pot. It's simple, delicious, and maybe even kind of healthy. Will eating it make you more like Emily Mariko? Possibly. But it might make you more like Tim Anderson. You have been warned!

INGREDIENTS

- 300 g (10½ oz/1⅓ cups) rice
- 360 ml (12 fl oz/1½ cups) water
- 2 tablespoons soy sauce
- 2 tablespoons sake
- 2 tablespoons mirin
- 1 teaspoon dashi powder
- 1 heaped tablespoon dried hijiki or wakame
- 2 tablespoons Sriracha sauce
- ½ teaspoon sesame oil
- 100 g (3½ oz) smoked mackerel, tinned tuna, or hot smoked salmon or trout
- 100 g (3½ oz) kimchi, drained and chopped
- 1 tablespoon sesame seeds
- 2 tablespoons mayonnaise
- 2 sheets nori, each cut into 6 pieces, or 2 packets Korean nori

METHOD

Combine the rice, water, soy sauce, sake, mirin, dashi powder, dried seaweed, Sriracha and sesame oil in a rice cooker or saucepan and stir. Cook according to your rice cooker's instructions or the stovetop instructions opposite. At the end of cooking, fold through the fish, kimchi and sesame seeds until well mixed. You can also fold through the mayo, or have it on top of the rice – whichever you prefer.

Serve with the nori on the side, which you can use to pick up little parcels of rice to shove in your gob (in a chic and healthy way).

MAKE IT VEGAN

Use crumbled smoked tofu instead of the fish, kombu dashi powder, and vegan mayo and kimchi.

'ASIAN' SLAW (A.K.A. SUMIKO ENDOW'S INSTANT RAMEN SALAD) ✯ ❦

SERVES 4

The whole idea of 'Asian slaw' is absurd – clearly the invention of people looking at Asia from a distance, making it small, as things appear when they're far away. But of course, cabbage-based salads do exist in Asia and the Asian diaspora – *Asian slaws*, if you will – and this is (kind of?) one of them. It's based on a recipe from my own family recipe book for something called 'Aunt Lynne's Sumi Salad'. My Aunt Lynne is as Asian as a tater tot casserole, but of course it's not *her* recipe anyway. Sumi salad was actually invented by Japanese-American Sumiko Endow, who published the recipe in a Santa Barbara community cookbook in the early eighties. Sure enough, that recipe is almost identical to the one in my family cookbook. How do I know this? Because Sumiko's daughter, Sandy Goe, wrote about it on her Substack – look it up!

The cleverest innovation in Sumiko's salad is the use of broken-up bits of instant ramen as crunchy little croutons. Make sure you use actual instant ramen for this – not dried ramen, rice noodles or anything else. Instant ramen is flash-fried, so it's cooked out and pleasantly crisp. You also use the ramen's seasoning packet, so make sure it's the cheap powdered kind rather than a concentrated paste.

INGREDIENTS

- 1 packet instant ramen (use a vegan version to keep it vegan)
- 50 g (1¾ oz/generous ½ cup) flaked (slivered) almonds
- juice of 1 lime
- 2 tablespoons sesame oil
- 2 tablespoons rice vinegar
- 2 tablespoons mirin
- 2 tablespoons sugar
- 1 tablespoon soy sauce
- 1 tablespoon tahini
- ¼ white cabbage
- ¼ red cabbage
- 2 spring onions (scallions), finely sliced
- 2 cm (¾ in) chunk of fresh root ginger, peeled and finely shredded
- 1 red chilli, deseeded and thinly sliced
- 1 carrot, julienned
- 1 tablespoon sesame seeds
- leaves from 1–2 sprigs of mint, roughly torn
- a handful of coriander (cilantro), roughly chopped

METHOD

Preheat the oven to 180°C (350°F/gas 4).

Open up the ramen packet and remove the seasoning sachet. Keep the noodles in the packet and smash them up into irregular bits – there should be some larger, crouton-like chunks, and many smaller noodle shards. Place the broken noodles onto a baking tray along with the flaked almonds, and bake for about 8 minutes, tossing them halfway through, until the nuts are golden brown. Remove from the oven and leave to cool.

Combine the ramen seasoning with the lime juice, sesame oil, vinegar, mirin, sugar, soy sauce and tahini in a jar. Shake well to mix and dissolve the sugar and soup powder. Slice the cabbages as thinly as possible (use a mandoline if you have one), then combine in a large mixing bowl with all of the rest of the vegetables and the sesame seeds and herbs. Just before serving, add the almonds, noodles and herbs, and toss with the dressing.

Karifurawā to Batā Bīnzu Karē Doria
カリフラワーとバタービーンズカレードリア

CAULIFLOWER & BUTTER BEAN CURRY GRATIN

SERVES 4
AS A SIDE OR 2 ON
ITS OWN

Doria are rice gratins, a yōshoku favourite dating back to the 1930s. Traditionally, they are made with white sauce, but there are also versions made with curry – a variant sometimes called yaki-curry. This recipe, using cauliflower, is what you'd get if a curry and cauliflower cheese had a baby. Great as a side dish, but with the addition of butter beans, it makes a very satisfying vegetarian main.

INGREDIENTS

- 1 medium head (450–500 g/1 lb–1 lb 2 oz) cauliflower, cut into florets
- salt, to taste
- 2 portions curry roux (about 30–50 g/1–1¾ oz, depending on the brand you have – check the instructions on the box)
- 300–350 ml (10–12 fl oz/1¼–1½ cups) water
- a little butter, for greasing
- 2 portions cooked rice (from 150 g/5½ oz/ generous ⅔ cup uncooked weight)
- 1 x 400g (14 oz) tin butter (lima) beans, drained and rinsed and drained again (optional)
- 150 g (5½ oz) medium Cheddar, Edam, mozzarella (any good, not-too-strong melting cheese), sliced or grated
- crispy onions and Japanese pickles, to garnish (optional)

METHOD

Boil, steam or microwave the cauliflower until just tender, but with plenty of bite – about 4–5 minutes depending on the cooking method. Drain the cauliflower well, then season it with a little salt.

Prepare two portions of curry sauce according to the instructions on the box. For a standard 90–100 g (3¼–3½ oz) box of roux, this usually entails dissolving half of the box into 300–350 ml (10–12 fl oz/1¼–generous 1⅓ cups) simmering water (you can skip the instructions about adding onions or meat or any other veg).

Preheat the oven to 200°C (400°C/gas 6). Grease a 20 cm (8 in) gratin dish or baking dish with a little butter.

Scoop the rice into the bottom of the prepared dish, packing it tightly, so the sauce doesn't drip down into it too much – you want a distinct layer of sauce. Place the blanched cauliflower on top of the rice in an even layer along with the butter beans (if using), then pour over the curry sauce. Top with the cheese, then bake for 20–25 minutes until well browned.

Serve piping hot, garnished with crispy onions and pickles, if you like. Fukujin-zuke are the classic choice, but pickled ginger is also delicious.

MAKE IT VEGAN

Use plant butter and vegan cheese – anything mild and melty will do.

Mūru-gai to Asupara no Zōsui
ムール貝とアスパラの雑炊

MUSSEL, WAKAME & ASPARAGUS RICE SOUP ✯ ❦

SERVES 4 GENEROUSLY

This is *zōsui*, a rice soup often made by adding cooked rice to the broth that remains at the end of a hotpot. But it can also be made from scratch, and can take almost anything. It is not to be confused with *okayu* (rice porridge); the grains should be distinct, not broken down. This version uses mussels, which release their own delicious dashi to flavour the broth. Clams will work too, if you can get good ones. And if you're a stickler for seasonality and there's no good asparagus going, any similar green vegetable will do, such as frozen peas or chopped green beans.

INGREDIENTS

- 1 kg (2 lb 4 oz) mussels
- 4 tablespoons sake or white wine
- a knob of butter
- 2 garlic cloves, smashed and thinly sliced
- 1 cm (½ in) chunk of fresh root ginger, peeled and finely chopped
- 1 litre (34 fl oz/4¼ cups) dashi, fish stock or light chicken stock
- 1 tablespoon dried wakame
- 4 spring onions (scallions), sliced
- 150–200 g (5½–7 oz) asparagus, trimmed as needed and cut into 1 cm (½ in) pieces
- 2 portions cooked rice (from 150 g/5½ oz/ generous ⅔ cup uncooked)
- salt or miso, to taste
- a little chopped flat-leaf parsley or dill

METHOD

Discard any open or broken mussels, remove their stringy 'beards' and rinse them well under cold water. Place in a saucepan with the sake or wine and bring to the boil with a lid on the pan. Steam for 5–6 minutes, tossing the mussels occasionally, until they have all opened and steamed through. Remove from the heat, then pick the mussel meat from the shells and set aside. Reserve the liquid.

In a separate saucepan, melt the butter over a medium-high heat. Add the garlic and ginger and cook for a few minutes to soften, then tip in the mussel juice through a fine sieve (strainer) to catch any grit or bits of shell. Add the dashi and bring to a high simmer, then add the wakame, spring onions and asparagus. Cook for 3–4 minutes until just cooked through but still firm. Stir in the rice and bring back up to a simmer. Taste and adjust seasoning as needed with salt or a bit of miso. Switch off the heat and stir through the mussel meat and chopped herbs.

MAKE IT VEGAN

Did you know that some vegans consider bivalves to be fair game, because they're immobile and non-sentient? No different from plants, I guess. So some of my vegan friends eat mussels, but some of them think this is appalling. It's up to you – you can either leave them out or replace them with oyster mushrooms. You'll have to bump up the seasoning if you don't use them, because mussels are naturally salty. Use plant butter and kombu dashi.

'CORNISH PASTY' RICE

SERVES 3–4

A little while ago, I bought a swede (rutabaga). Lord knows why. I guess I hadn't cooked swede in a while and fancied a little change of routine. The excitement never stops in the Anderson household!

A swede is a large and uncooperative vegetable, which is to say I wound up with more swede than I knew what to do with. But inspiration struck while I was munching on a pasty at Manchester Piccadilly station. The filling of a Cornish pasty is delicious, but I personally think (and I do not apologise to the people of Cornwall for saying this) that it would be better with rice as opposed to pastry. And so, the pasty takikomi gohan was born: steamy Japanese rice cooked with beef, onions, potatoes, and our grumpy old friend, swede.

INGREDIENTS

- 300 g (10½ oz/1⅓ cups) rice
- 4 tablespoons mirin
- 4 tablespoons sake
- 2 tablespoons soy sauce (ideally usukuchi)
- ¼ teaspoon salt, plus more to taste (if you like)
- quite a lot of black pepper
- 250 ml (8 fl oz/1 cup) water
- 3 coin-sized slices of fresh root ginger (optional)
- 10 cm (4 in) square piece of kombu (optional)
- 1 onion, diced
- 1 potato (about 150 g/5½ oz), washed and diced
- 150 g (5½ oz) swede (rutabaga), peeled and diced
- 400 g (14 oz) minced (ground) beef (this needs to be lean, or the dish will be quite greasy)
- a pat of salted butter (optional)

METHOD

Wash the rice well, then combine it in a saucepan or rice cooker with the mirin, sake, soy sauce, salt, pepper and measured water. Add the ginger and kombu (if you've got 'em) and nestle them into the rice, then top with the onion, potato, swede and mince (no need to break it up). Cook according to the instructions on page 100.

When the rice is done, remove the kombu and ginger, then fold the vegetables and mince through the rice, breaking up the mince as you go. If you like, mix in a little butter, then taste and adjust the seasoning as needed with salt and pepper. This is also nice with chilli oil.

Kinoko Chīzu Ramen
きのこチーズラーメン

CHEESY MUSHROOM RAMEN ✯

SERVES 1

This is essentially a hybrid of ramen and mac and cheese – filth, perhaps, but delicious filth. Perfect for those moments when only instant ramen can fill the void within us ... but we also want cheese.

INGREDIENTS

- 1 packet instant ramen (any flavour)
- 250 ml (8 fl oz/1 cup) water
- 150 g (5½ oz) oyster or (destemmed) shiitake mushrooms, roughly torn
- 2 slices processed cheese (do not substitute with 'real' cheese, it won't emulsify into the soup)
- 40 g (1½ oz) Cheddar cheese, grated
- black pepper and/or chilli (hot pepper) flakes, to taste
- a handful of chives, thinly sliced

METHOD

Place the ramen noodles and their seasoning packet(s) in a saucepan along with the water. Bring to the boil and cook until the noodles are al dente, adding the mushrooms about halfway through cooking – you'll have to toss the noodles occasionally, because you're using less water than usual. Once the noodles are cooked but still quite firm, stir in the processed cheese until it melts completely, then stir in the Cheddar cheese and remove from the heat. Mix well to ensure there are no lumps of cheese, then tip into a bowl, season to taste with black pepper or chilli flakes and garnish with the chives.

Karikari Chīzu nose Hamu Tamago Hōrensō Soba
カリカリチーズのせハム卵ほうれん草そば

SOBA WITH HAM, EGG, SPINACH & CRISPY COMTÉ

SERVES 2

French and Japanese food culture have several commonalities. A respect for craft. An appreciation of terroir. A superiority complex. And buckwheat. The nutty grain is perhaps best known as the key ingredient in galettes Bretonnes, which is what has inspired this recipe, borrowing ham, egg and cheese from France and introducing it to Japan's beloved buckwheat noodle.

INGREDIENTS

- 30 g (1 oz) Comté or Gruyère cheese, grated
- 500 ml (17 fl oz/2 cups) dashi
- 3–4 tablespoons soy sauce
- 2 tablespoons mirin
- 2 eggs
- 1 tablespoon rice vinegar (optional)
- 200 g (7 oz) soba noodles
- 2 very big handfuls of spinach
- 2 big slices of ham
- 1 spring onion (scallion), thinly sliced
- a couple of pinches of sesame seeds
- shichimi, to taste (optional)

METHOD

Place the cheese in two little mounds in a non-stick pan. Set over a medium-high heat and cook until the cheese melts, then turns a rich bronze all over. Remove each cheese tuile from the pan and drain on paper towels.

Combine the dashi, soy sauce and mirin and bring to a simmer in either a saucepan or the microwave. The eggs can be either raw, poached or soft-boiled and peeled. If you're poaching them, add the vinegar to the poaching water to help them set, and drain the eggs well on paper towels before adding to the soup.

Cook the soba according to the package instructions – keep an eye on the pot and don't boil it too rapidly, because it has a tendency to boil over. As soon as the soba is done, chuck the spinach in the pot, then drain immediately – the residual heat will wilt the spinach. Rinse the noodles and spinach under running water to remove the excess starch, then transfer to noodle bowls. Pour over the hot broth and garnish with the eggs, ham (folded in half if necessary to fit into the bowl better), spring onion, sesame seeds and cheese tuiles. Add shichimi, if you want a little spice.

Kunsei Nishin Soba
燻製ニシンそば

KIPPER SOBA ✯

SERVES 2

This dish is inspired by the classic nishin soba, a rustic dish of herring braised in soy sauce and mirin on soba noodles. Fresh herring is not always easy to get, but luckily, kippers are – and they're delicious, easy to cook, and cheap as chips. Or cheap as fish, as it were. They're an excellent alternative to fresh herring, and the broth here is generously dosed with mirin to replicate the sweetness of the original nishin soba.

INGREDIENTS

- 500 ml (17 fl oz/2 cups) Katsuo Dashi (page 23)
- 4 tablespoons mirin
- 1 tablespoon Demerara sugar
- 3–4 tablespoons soy sauce
- 1–2 kippers
- a handful of mangetout (snow peas) or snap peas
- 2 portions (180–200 g/6–7 oz) soba noodles
- 1 spring onion (scallion), thinly sliced
- a few small sprigs of flat-leaf parsley or dill
- a pinch of sansho or a dash of ponzu, to finish (optional)
- 2 eggs, poached or soft-boiled (optional)

METHOD

Combine the dashi, mirin, sugar and soy sauce in a saucepan and bring to a simmer. Taste and adjust the seasoning with additional soy sauce, if you like, bearing in mind the fish itself will be quite salty.

Grill (broil) the kippers on high until the skin is well browned and crisp, then set aside to cool slightly. When the kippers are cool enough to handle, remove their dorsal fin bones and chop or break them into chopstick-friendly chunks.

Prepare a large pot of boiling water. Toss the mangetout into the water and blanch for 1 minute, then remove with a slotted spoon and set aside. Cook the soba according to the package instructions, then rinse under cold water to remove excess starch.

Divide the soba between two noodle bowls, then top with the kippers, mangetout, spring onion and parsley or dill. Pour over the hot dashi and serve with sansho and/or ponzu at the table to add a little freshness (if you like). Runny poached or boiled eggs are also an amenable addition, especially for breakfast.

'NDUJA & FENNEL SEED UDON ☆

SERVES 2

This is an incredibly quick way to get your spicy-oily noodle kick. Three ingredients, about five minutes of cooking, and the flavour is like pizza, in udon form. Embellish this however you like – it's nice with spinach, mushrooms or artichoke hearts.

INGREDIENTS

- 75 g (2½ oz) 'nduja
- 1 heaped teaspoon fennel seeds
- 2 portions of udon noodles, par-cooked according to the packet instructions
- a few leaves of fresh basil and/or grated Parmesan, to garnish (optional)

METHOD

Place the 'nduja in a frying pan and set over a medium-high heat. Break it up into small chunks and when it starts to melt into a scary red puddle, add the fennel seeds and let them sizzle for 1–2 minutes. Add the par-cooked udon and sauté for a few minutes to coat the noodles (a splash of the udon cooking water, or just tap water, may help to liquefy the 'nduja and form a sauce).

Dish up and garnish with fresh basil and grated Parmesan, if you've got it.

BAKED CRABBY UDON ✭

SERVES 2

This is a simple but indulgent udon dish masquerading as a cheesy pasta bake, chock full of crab meat. It is very expensive, but also very delicious – something for payday. Treat yourself! (Or use tuna instead.)

INGREDIENTS

- 200 ml (7 fl oz/scant 1 cup) single (light) cream
- 50 ml (1¾ fl oz/3½ tablespoons) water
- 30 g (1 oz/2 tablespoons) miso
- 20 g (¾ oz) Parmesan, grated
- 1 teaspoon Old Bay, Cajun seasoning or similar spice mix
- 1 teaspoon katsuo dashi powder
- a few grinds of black pepper
- 200–300 g (7–10½ oz) crab meat (white, or 50:50 white and dark)
- 4 portions fresh or frozen udon noodles (about 800–900 g/1 lb 12 oz–2 lb, depending on the brand), parboiled and drained
- 150 g (5½ oz) Emmental, medium Cheddar, Edam, or similar melting cheese, grated
- 20–25 g (¾–1 oz/⅓ cup) panko
- quite a lot of chives, thinly sliced
- Tabasco sauce or similar, to serve (optional)

METHOD

Preheat the oven to 180°C (350°F/gas 4).

Combine the cream, water, miso, Parmesan, spice mix, dashi powder and pepper in a bowl, and whisk well to combine, ensuring there are no lumps of miso. Stir in the crab.

Place the udon into one large or two medium gratin dishes, then pour over the crab mixture. Give it a mix to work the sauce through the noodles, then scatter over the cheese and then the panko. Bake for 30–35 minutes until bubbling and browned.

Garnish with the chives and mix well before tucking in. For me, this likes a lot of Tabasco – have it ready on the table, if you wish.

HOT
SAUCE

木綿豆腐

CHAPTER 6

豆
腐

TOFU

ARE YOU KEEPING SCORE? BECAUSE I AM:

CHINA	CLEARSPRING
4	5

And here they are again, because TOFU (豆腐), like soy sauce and miso, originally comes from China, arriving in Japan via envoys during the Tang Dynasty. And for a good brand, Clearspring is, once again, a good choice.

Now let me back it up a bit: Chinese tofu, and indeed most tofu manufactured and sold in the West, is a bit different from Japanese tofu. This isn't to say it isn't good, but like so many Japanese ingredients, it's just better to buy actual Japanese brands because it's easier to ensure you're getting the right thing. Both Chinese tofu and Western brands of tofu can be so different in terms of texture, I'm not even sure they'd work in these recipes.

There are several types of tofu just within the realm of Japanese cuisine, but for our purposes we only need to know two: COTTON (MOMEN / 木綿) and SILKEN (KINUGOSHI / 絹ごし). The English names are direct translations, and they do a pretty good job of expressing their textures. Apparently there is a misconception that these names refer to the materials used to filter the solids out of the soy milk, but in fact, the way each type of tofu is made is more or less the same: cook soy beans and blend them to make a milk, strain out the fibre from the milk, add coagulant (*nigari* / 苦汁) to curdle the proteins, and set. The difference between cotton and silken is that silken uses a much thicker soy milk and is allowed to set into a solid (but delicate) block, without pressing. For cotton, the curds are removed from the whey and pressed to expel water, making the finished product firmer and denser but also less smooth on the palate. By the way, both are fairly easy (if a bit time-consuming) to make at home, if you want to have a go. Warm, freshly set tofu is a rare delight.

Note that FIRMNESS DOES NOT INDICATE THE TYPE OF TOFU – IT ONLY TELLS YOU THE FIRMNESS, which has to do with the extent of pressing (in cotton tofu) as well as the density of coagulated proteins. Firmness levels are essentially sub-categories of the two main types of tofu, so you need to make sure you're getting the right kind. As far as I know, I don't think firmness is actually standardised or regulated, so it's down to each individual manufacturer's discretion, and therefore actual density varies even at the same firmness level across brands. Some brands even make up their own categories, like 'super firm.' Do not trust any recipe that simply indicates 'firm' or 'soft' tofu – the author is withholding vital information. YOU MUST KNOW WHETHER YOU NEED COTTON OR SILKEN, BECAUSE THEY ARE SO DIFFERENT!

Silken tofu is sold ambient, in Tetra-paks. The tofu is actually set inside the container, so it slides out intact, in pleasing pillow- or brick-like shapes. This tofu has a velvety, custard-like texture and delicate structure, so it is not good for aggressive cooking, such as stir-frying. It is best served cold, or gently simmered or poached. It also blends beautifully into sauces (such as Vegan Japanese Mayo, page 201) or desserts (like Tofumisu, page 134).

Cotton tofu is sold refrigerated, because unlike silken tofu, the process of making it can't be done in a hermetically sealed, self-contained environment. It has to be set in a separate vessel, strained, pressed and then re-packaged, usually in its own whey. Somewhat annoyingly, cotton tofu is rarely labelled as such; it's kind of the default tofu, and indeed, Japanese Wikipedia says that in English, cotton tofu is just called 'regular tofu'. But if you're not sure, the clue is in the packaging. Room-temp Tetra-paks = silken. Refrigerated plastic containers = cotton.

In terms of brands, it's hard to go wrong with silken. CLEARSPRING is my favourite, with a gorgeous, crème caramel-like texture, but its 'beany' flavour is quite pronounced. If you want something more neutral, MORINAGA, J-BASKET and YUTAKA are all good choices. For cotton tofu, some of my favourite brands are HOUSE and SHIZEN NO MEGUMI. Smoked and marinated tofu are generally not used in Japanese cooking, but some of them are pretty tasty and would work well in dishes where stronger flavours are amenable, such as Tofu Miso Katsu (page 124).

Many recipes call for 'draining' tofu (mizu-kiri / 水切り, literally 'water-cutting') before using it, by microwaving it to expel water or by letting it sit in a bowl overnight in the refrigerator with a weight on top of it. This is usually unnecessary – if your tofu has too much water in it, in most situations the simplest solution is to just choose something firmer. However, draining silken tofu does help to make it more solid and easier to handle, especially if you want to cook with it, as you might in hotpots or deep-fried dishes. With any type of tofu, I usually pat its surface dry with a clean cloth before cooking – this helps it brown more easily in fried dishes, and take marinades more readily.

Beyond these basics, there are many, many other types of tofu to try, and many ways to use them. This guide, and these recipes, are just an introduction. So go forth – a great tofu adventure awaits you!

Tōfu no Misokatsu
豆腐の味噌カツ

TOFU MISO KATSU ✯ ❦

SERVES 2

Miso katsu is a speciality of Nagoya, home to the famous Hatchō miso that features in the dish's sauce. It is exactly what you might guess it is from the name: tonkatsu, smothered in a sauce of dark red miso, dashi and other seasonings. It's excellent with pork, of course, but it works with basically any protein, and it is a nice match for the mellow beany flavour of tofu.

INGREDIENTS

- 4 tablespoons very dark red miso, such as Hatchō or brown rice miso
- 4 tablespoons sake
- 4 tablespoons honey or maple syrup
- 2 tablespoons mirin
- 2 tablespoons water
- ¼ teaspoon dashi powder
- ½ teaspoon grated fresh root ginger (optional)
- a dash of Worcestershire sauce (optional)
- 1 block (300–400 g/10½–14 oz) medium or firm (cotton) tofu (smoked tofu is also tasty), patted dry
- salt, pepper and MSG, to taste
- 50 g (1¾ oz/scant ½ cup) plain (all-purpose) flour
- 100 ml (3½ fl oz/scant ½ cup) water
- about 100 g (3½ oz/1¾ cups) panko
- vegetable oil, for frying
- sesame seeds, to garnish

METHOD

Combine the miso, sake, honey or maple syrup, mirin, water, dashi powder, ginger and Worcestershire sauce (if using) in a saucepan and whisk well, until no lumps of miso remain. Bring to a simmer and cook for a few minutes to cook off the alcohol from the sake. Don't let the sauce reduce. Remove from the heat and leave to cool.

Cut the tofu in half to form two rectangular 'cutlets', and season each one with a pinch of salt, pepper and MSG. Whisk together the flour and water to make a batter, then dip each tofu katsu into it, then dredge in the panko to coat.

Pour enough oil into a frying pan to come up to a depth of about 5 mm (¼ in), then set over a high heat. When the oil is shimmering and feels hot when you hold your hand above its surface, lower in the tofu katsu and fry for about 8–10 minutes, turning occasionally, until golden brown and crisp all over. Drain on paper towels, then slice and serve with the miso sauce spooned over the top. Garnish with sesame seeds and enjoy with rice and vegetables.

MAKE IT VEGAN

Use maple syrup and omit the Worcestershire sauce.

OFFICIAL BEER
SUPER
DRY
Asahi
0.0%
330ml

Tōfu Gyōza no Rāyu Chīzu Yaki
豆腐餃子のラー油チーズ焼き

CHILLI CHEESE-CRUSTED TOFU GYOZA ✯ ❦

SERVES 1–2

This recipe is kind of a cheat – it calls for ready-made frozen tofu gyoza, but if you have tofu already, you can by all means make it from scratch. There's a pretty good recipe for tofu gyoza in (shameless plug) *Vegan JapanEasy*. The idea here, of frying them in chilli oil, came from egg wizard Ed Smith, who posted a recipe for eggs fried in chilli oil and sesame. I use cheese as well, because cheese is always an upgrade.

INGREDIENTS

- 1 tablespoon chilli oil (just the oil, not the solids)
- 20–25 g (¾–1 oz) medium Cheddar or similar cheese, grated
- 1 tablespoon mixed white and black sesame seeds (optional)
- 10 frozen tofu gyoza (or any kind of gyoza really)
- 75–100 ml (2½–3½ fl oz/5 tablespoons–scant ½ cup) water
- Gyoza Dip (page 199), to serve

METHOD

Pour the chilli oil into a non-stick pan and scatter over the cheese and sesame seeds (if using). Set over a high heat, then add the gyoza, flat-side down/seam-side up. Arrange them prettily – I like to make a nice pinwheel. Once the cheese has melted and everything is sizzling furiously, tip in the water and place a lid on the pan. Steam for 5 minutes, then remove the lid and let the liquid evaporate completely – the pan should look completely dry, except for a slick of cheesy chilli oil.

Once the water has evaporated, start to tease the crust away from the sides of the pan with a flexible spatula. If the cheese is gooey or sticky, let it cook for a little while longer to solidify and try again. Slide the spatula all around the underside of the gyoza to release them from the pan, then remove from the heat and invert the pan onto a plate – be careful of hot oil!

Serve with cold beer and gyoza dip on the side.

MAKE IT VEGAN

Simply swap the cow's cheese for plant cheese.

VEGAN STUFFED SHELLS WITH TOFU-MISO 'RICOTTA' ☆ ❦

SERVES 4

This recipe features a fake, plant-based 'ricotta' filling, which (if you'll allow me to boast and cuss for a moment) absolutely ファッキング nails the brief. The combination of tofu and miso gets at that tangy, creamy cheese flavour beautifully (see also: Vegan Matcha-Miso Double Cheesecake, page 175), an ideal partner to the sweet, rich tomato sauce.

INGREDIENTS

- 4 tablespoons olive oil
- 2 onions, finely chopped
- 5 garlic cloves, finely chopped
- 2 tablespoons tomato paste
- 30 g (1 oz/2 tablespoons) red miso
- 1 teaspoon dried oregano
- many grinds of black pepper, to taste
- 2 x 400 g (14 oz) tins finely chopped tomatoes (or 800 g/1 lb 12 oz/generous 3 cups) passata
- about 200 ml (7 fl oz/scant 1 cup) water
- salt, to taste
- 1 bunch (30 g/1 oz) basil, destemmed and torn or roughly chopped
- 400 g (14 oz) frozen spinach, thawed
- 400 g (14 oz) firm (cotton) tofu
- 60 g (2 oz/¼ cup) white miso
- a few gratings of nutmeg
- a little white pepper
- about 24 conchiglioni (giant pasta shells – roughly 180 g/6 oz)
- Shichimi Pangrattato, to garnish (optional)

NOTE

You may end up with some leftover tofu filling. This is delicious on its own, worked through pasta with a splash of pasta water to thin it, or on sourdough toast with tomatoes.

METHOD

Pour the olive oil into a wide casserole, cast-iron pan, or similar stove-to-oven cooking vessel that will fit a lot of pasta shells. Set over a medium-high heat and tip in the onions and all but one of the garlic cloves. Sauté until translucent, soft and a little bit brown, then add the tomato paste and red miso, smashing it into the oil with a spatula to break up the miso. Add the oregano and black pepper, then the tinned tomatoes and half a tin-full of water. Stir well. Reduce the heat to medium and simmer for about 20 minutes until the sauce is … saucy (it's okay if it's a little watery, because the pasta will absorb water as it bakes). Taste the sauce and adjust the seasoning as you like with salt and pepper. Remove from the heat and stir in half of the basil.

Squeeze the spinach firmly to expel excess water, then transfer to a food processor or blender along with the tofu, white miso, nutmeg, white pepper, the remaining garlic clove and the rest of the basil. Blitz until smooth and creamy.

Preheat the oven to 180°C (350°F/gas 4).

Cook the pasta a minute less than stated on the package instructions. Drain well and rinse briefly under running water, until cool enough to handle. Fill each shell with a generous spoonful of the tofu mixture (a piping bag is useful for this) and nestle each one into the sauce, arranging them in a pretty flower pattern as you go. Bake for about 30 minutes until piping hot and lightly browned along the edges.

If you've got it, this is very nice garnished with Shichimi Pangratatto (page 25).

Hiyayakko no Arenji Yottsu
冷奴のアレンジ4つ

FOUR WAYS WITH CHILLED SILKEN TOFU ✯ ❦

SERVES 2, OR 4 IF PART OF A LARGER MEAL

Hiyayakko is simply chilled silken tofu, with stuff on it. What kind of stuff? All kinds of stuff! Things that season the tofu, introduce stronger flavours and firmer textures for contrast and balance, are best. For example: the classic toppings of soy sauce (salty), katsuobushi (fishy) and ginger (spicy), the impact of which are softened by the tofu cushion below. Because of the format's simplicity, the Japanese recipe internet is awash with creative twists on hiyayakko. Here are mine.

INGREDIENTS

All recipes use 300–350 g (10½–12 oz) firm or extra-firm silken tofu

METHOD

HIYAYAKKO 1: CLASSIC KATSUOBUSHI AND GINGER

Finely grate 10–15 g (½ oz) peeled fresh root ginger and stir it together with 2 tablespoons soy sauce. Pour this mixture over the chilled tofu and top with 1 sliced spring onion (scallion), 2 pinches of sesame seeds and a little mound of katsuobushi.

HIYAYAKKO 2: GRILLED NECTARINE WITH HONEY, SEEDS, LAVENDER AND MINT

Toast 1 heaped tablespoon pumpkin, sesame and/or sunflower seeds in a dry pan or hot oven until lightly browned, then tip onto a plate to cool. Cut 1 ripe nectarine into 8 wedges, then grill (broil) or blowtorch the wedges until they are lightly blackened all over. Place the nectarines back in the refrigerator while you finish the dish to chill them back down. Pick the leaves from 2–3 mint sprigs and tear them into pieces. Place the chilled silken tofu onto a serving dish and arrange the nectarines on top, then scatter over the seeds. Drizzle over 1 tablespoon honey and 1 tablespoon olive oil, then scatter over the mint. Finish with a squeeze of juice from ½ lemon, a liberal amount of flaky sea salt and a pinch of dried lavender buds, rubbed between your fingers (if you have it).

MAKE IT VEGAN

Where animal products are specified, they can be easily removed or substituted. Use nori instead of katsuobushi; maple syrup instead of honey; and plant-based mince or tofu in the magic mince.

NOTE

As silken tofu is sold at room temperature, you'll have to put it in the refrigerator ahead of time to get it nice and cold. Pat the tofu dry with paper towels before adding the toppings.

HIYAYAKKO 3: CUCUMBER, RADISHES AND TOMATO WITH WAFŪ DRESSING

Slice 2 baby cucumbers (or 5 cm/2 in chunk of regular cucumber) and 6 radishes very thinly. Gently massage the sliced vegetables with a generous amount of salt, then leave to sit for 20–30 minutes. Meanwhile, halve 6 cherry or baby plum tomatoes. Rinse the sliced veg well, then squeeze them to expel excess water. Toss them with the tomatoes, 6 tablespoons Sweet Onion and Ginger Dressing (page 191) and a handful of picked fresh herbs (tarragon, basil or shiso are nice). Pile everything on top of the chilled tofu and enjoy.

HIYAYAKKO 4: MAGIC MINCE, EGG YOLK, SPRING ONIONS AND CHILLI OIL

Finely shred 2 spring onions (scallions) and place in a bowl of iced water for 10–15 minutes so they curl up and become super-cold and crisp. Top the chilled tofu block with 50 g (1¾ oz) Magic Mince (page 47). Make a little well in the centre of the mince pile and carefully nestle 1 egg yolk into it. Drain the iced spring onions well, then pile them on top of the tofu along with a handful of chopped coriander (cilantro). Drizzle a spoonful of soy sauce and chilli oil all over and garnish with sesame seeds.

TOFUMISU ☆ ❦

SERVES UP TO 8

My son Felix is allergic to milk and eggs (and some nuts), which is mostly fine, but occasionally heartbreaking. When I think about how he can never have a jammy ramen egg, or has to eat only sorbet and never ice cream, I am overwhelmed with pathos. The same goes for tiramisu, one of the world's best desserts. No, not just desserts – one of the world's best *things*. A life without tiramisu is no life at all. So I made it my mission to work out a recipe for tiramisu that Felix could eat.

And after many trials (and many errors) – and help from 'School Night Vegan' Richard Makin's vegan ladyfinger recipe – I think I've cracked it. It may not be the way they make it at your favourite trattoria, but it's pretty good. And most important to me, it's Felix-approved!

INGREDIENTS

FOR THE VEGAN SPONGE

- 2 tablespoons vegetable oil, plus extra for oiling
- 150 g (5½ oz/⅔ cup) caster (superfine) sugar, plus extra for dusting
- 240 g (8½ oz/scant 2 cups) plain (all-purpose) flour
- 2 tablespoons cornflour (cornstarch)
- 1 tablespoon baking powder
- 1 teaspoon bicarbonate of soda (baking soda)
- a few shakes of salt
- 200 ml (7 fl oz/scant 1 cup) plant milk
- 1 tablespoon rice vinegar
- ½ teaspoon almond extract
- 100 ml (3½ fl oz/scant ½ cup) amaretto
- 100 ml (3½ fl oz/scant ½ cup) espresso or other very strong coffee (use decaf for kids)

FOR THE TOFU CREAM

- 600 g (1 lb 5 oz) firm or extra-firm silken tofu (Clearspring works best)
- 400 ml (14 fl oz/generous 1½ cups) vegan whipping cream
- 180 g (6 oz/1½ cups) icing (powdered) sugar
- 20 g (¾ oz/4 teaspoons) sweet white miso
- 2 tablespoons vanilla bean paste
- 1 teaspoon lemon juice
- 50 g (1¾ oz/3½ tablespoons) plant butter, melted and cooled slightly
- cocoa powder, as needed, for dusting

METHOD

This needs to set for 24 hours in the refrigerator, so start making it the day before you serve it. You'll also need an approximately 18 x 25 cm (7 x 10 in) baking tray, at least 6 cm (2½ in) deep.

Preheat the oven to 160°C (325°F/gas 3). Line the baking tray with lightly oiled baking paper and dust it with a little sugar.

For the sponge, combine the sugar, flour, cornflour, baking powder, bicarb and salt in a mixing bowl and stir well to combine. In a separate bowl or jug, combine the milk, vinegar, almond extract and vegetable oil. Tip the wet mix into the dry mix and stir quickly to combine. It's okay if the batter has some small lumps of flour – mix just until the batter comes together, with no dry patches.

Pour the batter into the lined tray and dust its surface with more sugar. Bake for 40 minutes until cooked through (use a toothpick to check) and golden on top. Remove from the oven and leave to cool. When it is completely cool, remove the sponge from the tin and cut all the way through it horizontally with a bread knife to obtain two thin layers of sponge (each about 1 cm/½ in deep). Cut each layer into batons, each about 2.5 cm (1 in) across.

Pour the amaretto into a small saucepan, bring to the boil to cook off the alcohol and let it reduce by half. Remove from the heat, then pour in the espresso and stir. Leave to cool while you prepare the tofu cream.

Combine all of the ingredients for the tofu cream, except the butter and cocoa powder, in the bowl of a stand mixer. Whip on full speed, pausing to scrape down the sides of the bowl with a spatula a couple of times at the beginning. Continue to whip until the mix is thick, smooth, light and airy – it will take about 5 minutes and it will not form peaks, but that's okay. When the mixture is whipped and voluminous, drizzle in the melted butter with the mixer still running to disperse it through the cream. At the end the texture should be halfway between whipped cream and custard – fluffy but pourable.

Pour about 2 tablespoons of the coffee mixture into the bottom of the same tin you baked the cakes in. Arrange half of the sponge fingers into the tin, then spoon some more coffee mixture onto each one, soaking them completely. Pour half of the whipped tofu cream on top, then lay the remaining sponge fingers on top of the cream layer. Spoon over more of the coffee mixture to soak, then add the remaining tofu cream on top.

Cover and chill in the refrigerator for at least 24 hours before serving – but it's best after about two days. Dust the surface with cocoa powder before chilling, or just before serving, or both, depending on what sort of texture and appearance you prefer. Any extra tofu cream that doesn't quite fit in the tin can be transferred to a separate container and set in the refrigerator – it will be like a little vanilla mousse!

SILKEN TOFU SMOOTHIES, THREE WAYS

ALL SERVE 2
(OR MAYBE JUST 1 IF THIS IS YOUR ENTIRE BREAKFAST)

Get your plant protein in, people! Occasionally, I end up with a frustrating little chunk of silken tofu left over in the refrigerator, and I don't know why it took me so long to realise that I can just whack it into a smoothie. Reconstituted with water, it basically just becomes soy milk, after all. Its amenable blandness means it works in any smoothie, but these are a few I really enjoy.

SMOOTHIE 1: CHERRY ALMOND MAPLE

Blend 100 g (3½ oz) silken tofu, 200 g (7 oz) frozen sweet cherries, 200 ml (7 fl oz/scant 1 cup) water or coconut water, 2 tablespoons maple syrup and 1 teaspoon almond extract until smooth.

SMOOTHIE 2: CUCUMBER GINGER MINT

Blend 100 g (3½ oz) silken tofu, ½ cucumber, 1–2 cm (½–¾ in) chunk of fresh root ginger (peeled), the leaves from about 6 sprigs of mint, 1 pear (cored, and peeled if you want to), juice of 1 lime and 120 ml (4 fl oz/½ cup) apple or pineapple juice.

SMOOTHIE 3: BIRTHDAY CAKE

Blend 100 g (3½ oz) silken tofu, 200 g (7 oz) strawberries, 200 ml (7 fl oz/scant 1 cup) water (or milk or fruit juice), 1 tablespoon vanilla bean paste and ½ teaspoon almond extract. Decorate (if you like) with whipped cream and sprinkles.

ゆず果汁
柚子こしょう

ポン酢

CHAPTER 7

柚子汁・ポン酢・柚子こしょう

YUZU JUICE, PONZU & YUZU KOSHŌ

YUZU (柚子・ゆず) is officially not cool anymore, because James Martin uses it. I have a lot of respect for James Martin, but not because he's a trend-setter, you know? Once James Martin is cooking with something, that means it's already transitioned from something your nephew cooks with to something your dad cooks with, from Waitrose to Aldi, from Ottolenghi to ... well, James Martin.

So yuzu's novelty may have worn off, but it is still wonderful stuff. Originally from – you guessed it – Tang Dynasty China, the yuzu is a hybrid of a mandarin and a knobbly lemon-like citrus fruit called the Ichang papeda. Yuzu's fragrance is both mandarin- and lemon-like, but it is also so much more – complex, floral and herbaceous. Its aroma compounds include:

LIMONENE
LEMONY, ORANGEY

PINENE
PINEY, LIME LEAFY

PHELLANDRENE
PEPPERY, MINTY

MYRCENE
HOPPY, THYME-Y, LEMONGRASSY, JUNIPER-Y

LINALOOL
LAVENDER-Y, BERGAMOT-Y

Yuzu produces a symphony of invigorating smells, with the floral character of neroli and bergamot, the fresh scent of lime and lemon-grass, and a woody-herbal note of pine and thyme. It is no wonder James Martin uses it – it's irresistible!

But here's the rub: most of this aroma comes from yuzu peel, where the essential oils are. In Japan, where fresh yuzu is common, and good-quality dried or frozen peel is available when yuzu isn't in season, a tiny bit of zest can be used to perfume a bowl of soup or a piece of sushi. If you have fresh yuzu, this is the most effective way to add that signature yuzu flavour to your food. And while you can – occasionally – get fresh yuzu, it's pricey, rare, and its season is brief. If you are able to get some, I recommend preserving it as Ponzu (page 193), so you can enjoy it throughout the year.

You can also buy dried yuzu peel in various forms, but it's often under-powered in terms of aroma. You can get frozen peel, too, which again is a little bit flat compared to fresh fruit. So that leaves us with bottled juice, which is probably the best option – but it's expensive. Yuzu are dry little fruits with a lot of seeds and a lot of pith, so they don't yield much juice. But luckily, yuzu juice is strong stuff, so you don't usually need to use very much of it to make an impact. That is, provided you buy good yuzu juice.

How do you know you're getting good yuzu juice? For me, the easiest way is to buy it from a reputable shop, somewhere that focuses on flavour and provenance. The WASABI COMPANY, for example, has several premium varieties, and JAPAN CENTRE also has a good range. Some yuzu juice comes in large-format bottles, as big as 1.8 litres (60 fl oz). These may seem like good value, but I would advise against them. The aroma will start to fade over time, even in a sealed bottle, so unless you're getting through it very quickly, you'll end up with a lot of stale, sour, sub-par juice. You may also find yuzu juice that has salt added to help preserve it. This stuff is usually okay, but it can throw your seasoning out of whack, so just bear that in mind when you cook with it.

Having said all of this, sometimes to deliver a yuzu flavour you're better off bypassing the pure juice and using yuzu-based seasonings, namely PONZU (ポン酢) and YUZU KOSHŌ (柚子胡椒), which both capture yuzu oils beautifully while adding their own little something. Ponzu can be made from any sour citrus, usually blended with soy sauce (technically *ponzu-jōyu* / ポン酢醤油) and other seasonings for balance and preservation. Wasabi Company has some great ones, and good old CLEAR-SPRING is probably the best supermarket brand you'll find.

Yuzu koshō takes the already lively flavour of yuzu and ramps it up by pounding it into a paste with chillies and salt. It's pungent stuff, and while its heat isn't amenable to everything, it preserves yuzu's all-important essential oils better than any other product I know. It's great on its own, wherever a spicy-salty-citrussy kick is required (and excellent with chocolate), but I often use it in conjunction with ponzu or yuzu juice to provide a 'full fruit' yuzu flavour.

Ultimately, yuzu occupies the same kind of flavour space as more prosaic fruits like lemon and lime – it's there to freshen things up, make your mouth water and snap your senses into focus. But while yuzu is comparatively expensive, it's also irreplaceable – nothing else delivers quite the same aroma. Besides, its prohibitively high price might actually be a kind of benefit, because it will keep you from using it every day. If there's one thing yuzu should never be, it's boring or mundane. Use yuzu to keep things fresh – in more ways than one.

のんある
気分

PASSION FRUIT PONZU CEVICHE

SERVES 2

This is exactly what it sounds like: fresh fish pickled in tangy ponzu. The salt from the soy sauce seasons the fish perfectly as the acid from the citrus cures and flavours it. Note that because ponzu isn't as acidic as the pure citrus juice you'd use in a traditional ceviche, it's not as antimicrobial. This means your fish has to be spankin' fresh, and it's best practice to freeze it overnight before preparing.

INGREDIENTS

- 2 skinless, boneless, very fresh sea bream fillets or similar white fish (about 150–180 g/5½–6 oz in total)
- 6 tablespoons ponzu
- 1 teaspoon yuzu koshō
- pulp and seeds from 1 large or 2 small passion fruit
- ½ small red onion, thinly sliced
- 1 small mild red chilli, deseeded and thinly sliced
- about ½ teaspoon sesame oil
- a sprinkle of sesame seeds
- a few sprigs of coriander (cilantro), chopped

METHOD

Cut the fish into slices, no more than 1 cm (½ in) thick. Toss together with the ponzu, yuzu koshō, passion fruit, onion and chilli. Transfer to the refrigerator and leave to cure for 1 hour, then stir the mixture and leave for another hour.

To serve, place in a shallow bowl and garnish with a drizzle of sesame oil, the sesame seeds and chopped coriander.

FENNEL, CHICORY & ORANGE SALAD WITH YUZU-HONEY VINAIGRETTE ✯ ❦

SERVES 4

The fennel-chicory-orange combination in a salad feels very Ottolenghi/Nigel Slater ca. 2005 to me. But it still works! And our old friend yuzu matches all of them beautifully.

INGREDIENTS

- 1 medium fennel bulb
- salt, as needed
- 1 orange, segmented
- 2 heads chicory (endive), chopped
- 2 tablespoons yuzu juice
- 1 tablespoon soy sauce
- 1 tablespoon rice vinegar
- 1 tablespoon olive oil
- 1 tablespoon honey
- 1 teaspoon Dijon mustard
- 1 teaspoon yuzu koshō (optional)
- a grind or two of black pepper
- a few handfuls of toasted seeds or nuts (pine nuts or pumpkin seeds are nice)

METHOD

Slice the fennel very thinly – use a mandoline, if you have one. Toss the fennel with a very generous sprinkling of salt, then leave in the refrigerator for at least 30 minutes to wilt. Rinse the fennel under running cold water, then drain and squeeze the fennel firmly to expel excess water.

Place the fennel in a salad bowl along with the orange segments and chicory.

Combine all of the remaining ingredients, except the nuts or seeds, in a little jar and shake well to mix. Toss the salad with the dressing and garnish with the toasted seeds.

MAKE IT VEGAN

Swap the honey for maple or rice malt syrup.

Suika to Abokado no Sunomono
スイカとアボカドの酢の物

WATERMELON & AVOCADO SUNOMONO

SERVES AT LEAST 4

Sunomono ('vinegar things') occupy the borderlands between pickles and salads. The classic combination is cucumber and wakame, but the sunomono treatment can apply to anything that benefits from an invigorating sourness, like watermelon, a.k.a. big pink cucumbers. I originally chucked the avocado in here because I had an avocado that needed using up, and it was actually quite nice! So here it is.

INGREDIENTS

- salt, as needed
- 5 mini cucumbers, thinly sliced
- 2 tablespoons rice vinegar
- 2 tablespoons mirin
- 1 tablespoon yuzu juice (or lemon or lime juice)
- 400 g (14 oz) seedless watermelon, cut into bite-size chunks
- 1 mild chilli, deseeded and finely chopped
- 1 cm (½ in) chunk of fresh root ginger, peeled and finely chopped
- 1 avocado, stoned and diced
- 40–50 mint leaves, picked
- 1 tablespoon sesame seeds

METHOD

Gently massage a generous sprinkling of salt into the cucumber slices and set aside for 30 minutes to wilt. Combine the vinegar, mirin and citrus juice in a little jar and shake.

Rinse and drain the cucumbers well, then squeeze them out to expel excess water. Combine them with the watermelon, chilli, ginger and avocado, then dress with the vinegar mixture. This can be made and dressed about 1 hour in advance of serving, which will allow the ingredients to absorb the dressing, but any longer than this and they will start to lose their texture.

Just before serving, toss with the mint leaves and garnish with sesame seeds.

ASPARAGUS WITH YUZU BEURRE BLANC

SERVES 4

Shout out to my old chef Adam for this idea. Back at the restaurant, we would put on a weekly changing special with fish from Brixton Market, and he came up with this sauce to put on pan-fried seabass. It's just as tasty on robust veg, like asparagus. Add a poached egg and some toast and you've got yourself a primo breakfast.

INGREDIENTS

- 4 tablespoons sake
- 1 tablespoon yuzu juice
- 1 tablespoon white miso
- 100 g (3½ oz/scant ½ cup) butter, cubed
- 1½–2 teaspoons sugar
- finely ground white pepper or cayenne, to taste
- 400–500 g (14 oz–1 lb 2 oz) asparagus

METHOD

Bring the sake to the boil in a small saucepan. Boil until the liquid is reduced by about a quarter, then reduce the heat to low and whisk in the yuzu juice and miso. Add the butter, a few cubes at a time, stirring occasionally to slowly melt them into the liquid. Don't rush this, because the sauce may split if it melts too quickly. Add the sugar and a pinch or two of pepper or cayenne, then taste and adjust the seasoning as needed. (The sugar is just to balance the yuzu; the sauce shouldn't be sweet.) Remove from the heat, but cover the pan to keep it warm as you cook the asparagus.

Blanch the asparagus in salted boiling water for 2–4 minutes until tender but still crisp at the core. Drain well and transfer to plates, then pour over the sauce.

MAKE IT VEGAN

Use plant butter.

NOTE

This sauce is temperamental! If it gets too hot, it will separate; if it gets too cold, it also may separate, but it will come back together if you whisk it hard. Even if it can't be saved, you'll end up with a tasty yuzu-infused melted butter sauce, which does the job!

SMOKED MACKEREL SANDWICHES WITH WASABI-PONZU DRESSING ✯

SERVES 2

Gotta love smoked mackerel. There's almost no fish with a stronger flavour, which means it loves other strong flavours, like the wasabi, ponzu and fresh herbs in this big, drippy, elbows-on-the-table sandwich.

INGREDIENTS

- 1 medium or 2 small tomatoes, sliced about 4–5 mm (¼ in) thick
- 2 little cucumbers, sliced into planks about 4–5 mm (¼ in) thick
- salt and MSG, as needed
- 2 tablespoons ponzu
- 2 tablespoons mayonnaise
- 1 tablespoon wasabi
- 1 tablespoon olive oil
- 4 small or 2 big boneless smoked mackerel fillets (about 250 g/9 oz total)
- black pepper or not-too-hot chilli (hot pepper) flakes (such as gochugaru or pul biber), to taste
- a big handful each of fresh dill, mint and parsley
- 2 ciabatta rolls or 2 small baguettes (or 1 regular baguette, halved), cut open and lightly toasted

METHOD

Sprinkle the sliced tomatoes and cucumbers with salt and MSG and leave them to sit while you prepare the rest of the dish. Combine the ponzu, mayo, wasabi and olive oil and either stir well or shake them in a jar until a smooth vinaigrette is formed.

Grill (broil) the mackerel until the skin is crisp, then season with lots of pepper or chilli flakes.

Pat the cucumbers and tomatoes dry with paper towels. Lay a mound of fresh herbs onto the bottom slice of bread and pour over about half of the vinaigrette, then pile on the mackerel, tomatoes, cucumbers and another handful of herbs. Pour the remaining vinaigrette all over and close the sandwich. Enjoy warm and fresh, or wrap up tightly in baking paper and have cold later.

Burokkorī to Yuzu Koshō Mayo
ブロッコリーと柚子胡椒マヨ

BROCCOLI WITH YUZU KOSHŌ MAYO ✯

SERVES 2

This is an homage to the London food blogger's favourite side dish of 2012, served at Bone Daddies. It is extremely easy to make – and the mayo has lots of additional uses, so scale up the recipe, if you like.

INGREDIENTS

- 2 tablespoons mayonnaise
- 1 teaspoon yuzu koshō
- ½ teaspoon lime or yuzu juice
- water or dashi (from a powder, not the good stuff), as needed (about 500 ml/17 fl oz/2 cups)
- salt, as needed
- 200 g (7 oz) tenderstem or purple sprouting broccoli

MAKE IT VEGAN

Use Vegan Japanese Mayo (page 201).

METHOD

Stir together the mayo, yuzu koshō and lime or yuzu juice until well mixed.

Bring a saucepan full of water or dashi to the boil and add a few very big pinches of salt. Add the broccoli and cook for 3 minutes, until just tooth-tender, then drain well.

You can eat this warm, but I prefer it chilled – just put the broccoli in the refrigerator, uncovered, until cold. Serve with the mayo on the side, for dipping.

NO-CHURN YUZU-PEACH ICE CREAM ✯ ❦

MAKES ABOUT 600 ML (20 FL OZ/2½ CUPS)

This tastes kind of like a zingy lemon tart, in ice cream form. No peaches? This will take any fruit with a similar sweetness and texture: mango, melon or strawberries would all work.

INGREDIENTS

- 300 ml (10 fl oz/1¼ cups) whipping cream
- 120 g (4 oz/generous ⅓ cup) condensed milk
- 180 g (6 oz/½ cup) honey
- 4 tablespoons yuzu juice
- 1 big or 2 small ripe peaches, peeled and diced (or you can use tinned)

METHOD

Combine everything except the peaches in a large mixing bowl and use an electric whisk to whip the mixture until it is thick and airy. Fold in the peaches, then transfer to a container and place in the freezer for at least 4 hours, until frozen through.

MAKE IT VEGAN

You can use condensed coconut milk and vegan whipping cream for this, but it will make it taste like coconut.

カレー
カレールウ

CHAPTER 8

カレールウ

CURRY ROUX

If I had a time machine, I know exactly when and where I'd go: Japan, 1868. This was the year of the Meiji Restoration, which set in motion the official Westernisation, industrialisation and imperial expansion of Japan. It was a turbulent time, and I'd probably be killed one way or another, but not before I had a chance to experience modern Japanese food culture at the moment of its inception. This was when the country became fully engaged with Western and other foreign food cultures, and adopted them freely, localising them in ways that would become distinctly Japanese. Ramen, tonkatsu and *shokupan* were all Meiji developments, as was *karē raisu* (カレーライス): Japanese curry rice.

Curry was introduced to Japan by the British, who had already fully appropriated the dish from South Asia, Victorian-ising it with ingredients like bananas, dripping, honey and a roux, which would become a defining feature of Japanese curry. Curry caught on almost immediately, which is a little surprising considering both meat and spices were unfamiliar to Japanese people at the time. But the combination is what made it work; spices masked the odd, gamey smell of the meat, and at the same time made the dish feel exotic and cosmopolitan. It helped that curry was associated with the prowess of the British navy, and heavily promoted by the Japanese government to encourage people to eat more meat, to combat malnutrition and commodify by-products from Japan's nascent wool and leather industries.

By World War II, curry was an established part of a new 'national people's cuisine' (*kokuminshoku* / 国民食). This was initially a formalised set of dietary guidelines promoted by the imperial government, but later came to describe the kind of cheap, accessible comfort foods that people identified as their own. A contemporary equivalent is *B-kyū gurume* (B級グルメ, or B-grade gourmet), which similarly encompasses a range of filling, flavourful, affordable soul foods, including curry.

Curry's popularity broadened and deepened even further in the years after war, with the advent of packaged CURRY ROUX (KARĒ RUU / カレールウ). This allowed even the most unskilled of home cooks to make curry in an instant, and it was cheap. Curry roux became an indispensable household staple, as ubiquitous as rice and dashi powder.

And now, Japanese curry has bounced back to Britain. Driven primarily by Wagamama, katsu curry in particular has become a huge phenomenon across the UK, now even appearing on the menus of such unlikely institutions as Greggs and Wetherspoons. And after so many years of quite stupidly making Japanese curry from scratch at home (and yes, I've published several recipes to that end, for which I can only apologise), we have finally discovered and fully embraced curry roux: the easiest and most authentic way to make Japanese curry.

So, which roux to buy? This is really down to personal preference. I like JAVA. I like GOLDEN. I like YUTAKA. I don't much like Torokeru or Vermont. Take your pick – your choice may be more determined by dietary requirements than by flavour; for example, Vermont isn't vegan because it contains honey and cheese, and some other brands may contain milk or nuts or sesame seeds. This is also a situation where you should be careful not to be hoodwinked by non-Japanese brands. Many supermarkets now sell 'katsu curry' sauce or sauce bases that don't work the same way as real Japanese curry roux, and don't taste right. These can, as they say, get in the bin.

One thing to note about the recipes is that each curry brand varies a bit in terms of the viscosity of the sauce it produces. If anything turns out a bit too thin for your liking, you can reduce the water. If it's too thick, you can add more water, but then you'll have to add a touch of seasoning (salt, soy sauce or miso will do) to make up for the more diluted flavour. On that note, it's common to customise roux-based curry with additional seasonings, like hot sauce, ketchup, soy sauce, tonkatsu sauce, etc. – anything you like to make it your own.

One final point. I have said this many, many, many, MANY times before, but it bears repeating: KATSU CURRY IS NOT A TYPE OF CURRY. IT IS JAPANESE CURRY WITH A FRIED CUTLET ON IT. KATSU = CUTLET. No cutlet, no katsu curry!

Okay, I'm done. Have fun!

KATSU CURRY PARMO ✯

SERVES 4
VERY GENEROUSLY

A parmo is a Teeside speciality of breaded chicken topped with béchamel and molten cheese. It's insanely delicious, but it's the kind of dish you'll need a long nap after. You'll want pickles to go with this for a much-needed cut-through. The classic choice is fukujin-zuke, but I'd recommend something a bit sharper: pickled ginger. Both gari (the kind you have with sushi) or beni shōga (the red kind) will work.

INGREDIENTS

- 1 tablespoon butter
- 65 g (2¼ oz/½ cup) plain (all-purpose) flour
- 250 ml (8 fl oz/1 cup) milk
- ½ pack (45–50 g/1½–1¾ oz) curry roux
- 100 ml (3½ fl oz/scant ½ cup) water
- 120 g (4 oz/2 cups) panko
- 4 skinless and boneless chicken breasts
- salt, pepper and MSG, as needed
- vegetable oil, for shallow-frying
- 150 g (5½ oz) medium Cheddar or Red Leicester (or a mix of both), grated
- Japanese pickles, ideally pickled ginger or fukujin-zuke, as needed, to serve

METHOD

Melt the butter in a small saucepan over a medium-high heat and whisk in 15 g (½ oz/1¾ tablespoons) of the flour. Pour in the milk, a little at a time, whisking as you go, then bring to the boil while whisking frequently to form a smooth, thick sauce. Add the curry roux and whisk to dissolve and thicken even more. When the roux is completely dissolved, remove from the heat.

In a large bowl or dish, whisk together the water and the remaining flour to make a batter. Place the panko in a separate bowl or dish. Butterfly the breasts by cutting through them horizontally, almost all the way to the other side, so you can open them up like a book and lay them flat. Season them with salt, pepper and MSG. Dredge the seasoned chicken in the batter, then in the panko, pressing down on the breadcrumbs to ensure an even coating.

Preheat the grill (broiler) to medium. Pour enough oil into a wide pan to come up to a depth of about 1 cm (½ in) and set it over a medium-high heat. Every now and then, check its temperature by tossing some breadcrumbs into the oil. When they sizzle rapidly, the oil is hot enough. Carefully lower the chicken cutlets into the oil – you will likely only be able to cook two at a time. Cook for 5–6 minutes on each side until well browned and cooked through. Transfer the chicken to a wire rack set over a roasting tray. Spoon a generous amount of the curry sauce onto each chicken cutlet, then cover them in grated cheese and slide under the grill. Cook for about 5 minutes until the cheese is fully melted, bubbly and beginning to brown.

Serve piping hot, with pickles and rice, chips or salad.

Jinjābureddo Fūmi no Sūpu Karē
ジンジャーブレッド風味のスープカレー

'GINGERBREAD' SOUP CURRY WITH CHICKPEAS AND ROASTED BABY VEG ✯

SERVES 4 VERY GENEROUSLY

The addition of dried ginger to this curry roux-based soup came to me on a whim, and the result was marvellously gingerbread-like. The addition of squash called to mind pumpkin pie, giving the soup a Christmassy, comforting quality that I absolutely love. It's a great bowlful to enjoy on the sofa, under a blanket, on a cold and drizzly day.

INGREDIENTS

- 1 small butternut squash (700 g/1 lb 9 oz peeled weight), peeled, deseeded and cubed
- olive oil, as needed
- salt and chilli (hot pepper) flakes, as needed
- 4 pieces each: baby corn, okra, sweet baby peppers and baby courgettes (zucchini)
- 800 ml (27 fl oz/scant 3½ cups) water
- 1 pack (90–100 g/3¼–3½ oz) curry roux
- 2 tablespoons miso
- 1 teaspoon ground ginger
- 1 x 400 g (14 oz) tin chickpeas (garbanzos), drained
- plain yoghurt or sour cream, to taste
- a small handful of coriander (cilantro) and/or mint
- chilli oil (optional), to taste

METHOD

Preheat the oven to 200°C (400°F/gas 6).

Place the butternut squash on a baking tray and toss with a generous glug of olive oil, a sprinkle of salt and a little pinch of chilli flakes. On a separate tray, do the same with the other vegetables. Roast the squash for about 30 minutes, tossing once during cooking, until soft and well browned. Roast the other veg for 15–20 minutes until cooked, but still firm.

Meanwhile, combine the water, roux, miso and ginger in a saucepan and bring to the boil, stirring occasionally to dissolve the roux. When the squash is cooked, add about two-thirds of it to the curry and blend with a hand-held stick blender until smooth. Add the remaining squash and the chickpeas to the soup and bring back to a simmer.

To serve, ladle the soup into large bowls and place the roasted veg on top. Garnish with a little dollop of yoghurt and some chopped coriander and/or mint and, if you like, a little chilli oil. This soup is pretty substantial, but if you want more carbs it can be served with bread, potatoes or turmeric rice.

MAKE IT VEGAN

Use plant-based yoghurt or cream.

Ramu-Niku no Hanbāgu
ラム肉のハンバーグ

LAMB-BĀGU

SERVES 4

In Japan, store-bought curry is often embellished with all kinds of seasonings and spices – it is an endlessly customisable dish. This version adds a glug of ruby port and a little red miso to bring a rich sweetness, almost calling to mind a demi-glace. It pairs perfectly with lamb patties, a take on the classic Japanese (usually beef-based) *hanbāgu*, or hamburger steaks.

INGREDIENTS

- 1 tablespoon butter
- 1 onion, finely diced
- 2 garlic cloves, finely chopped
- 40 g (1½ oz/⅔ cup) panko
- 4 tablespoons milk
- ½ teaspoon dried mint, parsley or basil
- ¼ teaspoon ground cumin
- a pinch of chilli powder
- a generous pinch each of salt and pepper
- 500 g (1 lb 2 oz) minced (ground) lamb
- 120 ml (4 fl oz/½ cup) ruby port
- 1 tablespoon red miso
- 1 pack (90–100 g/3¼–3½ oz) curry roux
- 1 tablespoon olive or vegetable oil
- chopped flat-leaf parsley, to garnish

METHOD

Melt the butter in a frying pan over a medium heat. Add the onion and garlic and sauté until well browned, about 12 minutes. Remove from the heat and tip into a mixing bowl, then add the panko, milk, dried herbs, cumin, chilli powder and salt and pepper. Stir well, then leave for about 10 minutes so the onions cool and the panko softens in the milk. Add the lamb and work it through all of the seasonings with your hands. Form into four oblong patties.

Put the port and miso into a saucepan and bring to the boil. This will take the place of some of the water specified on the curry roux box, so add enough water to make up the total liquid required. Bring to the boil, then add the roux itself, whisking to dissolve, then remove from the heat.

Add the oil to the frying pan and set over a high heat. When the oil is very hot, lay in the lamb patties. Cook for about 4 minutes on each side until nicely browned. Towards the end of cooking, drain the excess fat from the pan, or mop it up with paper towels – too much oil will make the sauce split. Pour the port curry sauce into the pan and cover with a lid. Cook for a further 4–5 minutes, so the patties steam through and soften, and the sauce clings to their surface.

Serve with rice or taters (or both), garnished with a little fresh parsley.

Kīma Karē Pasuta
キーマカレーパスタ

KEEMA CURRY PASTA ✭ ❦

SERVES 4

This Bolognese-meets-curry feels like something the British should have invented, but of course it could only be from Japan, where both pasta and curry are culinary arenas in which pretty much everything is fair game. The sauce is quite sweet, so for me it needs Tabasco or sriracha, but my kids love it as is.

INGREDIENTS

- 2 tablespoons vegetable oil or butter
- 1 onion, finely diced
- 2 carrots, peeled and finely diced
- 400–500 g (14 oz–1 lb 2 oz) minced (ground) meat (whatever kind you like)
- 200 ml (7 fl oz/scant 1 cup) passata
- 300 ml (10 fl oz/1¼ cups) water (or a little more, as needed)
- ½ pack (45–50 g/1½–1¾ oz) curry roux
- 100 g (3½ oz) frozen peas
- soy sauce and hot chilli sauce, to taste
- 300 g (10½ oz) pasta (any kind, really)

METHOD

Heat the oil in a frying pan over a medium-high heat, add the onion and carrots and sauté until browned, about 8 minutes. Add the mince, break it up, and brown that as well, then add the passata and water and bring to the boil. Stir in the curry roux and let it dissolve and thicken the sauce. If it's too thick, add a splash more water. Add the frozen peas and cook for a few minutes to warm through, then taste the sauce and adjust the seasoning as you like with soy sauce and hot chilli sauce (if you need it).

Meanwhile, boil the pasta in salted water according to the packet instructions and drain well.

To serve, either toss the sauce through the pasta or just ladle it on top. Serve with more chilli sauce, to be used as needed.

MAKE IT VEGAN

Use vegan mince (soy mince or crumbled cotton tofu work well) or chopped mushrooms in place of the meat.

Bīgan Tsukemen
ビーガンつけ麺

RICH CURRY TSUKEMEN WITH STICKY OYSTER MUSHROOMS ✯

SERVES 4

Curry roux provides an excellent platform for tsukemen (dipping ramen), because tsukemen broth is typically thick and viscous in order to coat and cling to noodles. This is a vegan version, but it's so rich and filling you absolutely won't miss the meat.

INGREDIENTS

- ½ leek, cleaned, white and green parts separated
- 4 tablespoons chilli oil (just the oil – no bits), plus more to garnish
- 4 tablespoons miso
- 4 tablespoons tahini
- 1.2 litres (40 fl oz/5 cups) water
- 1 teaspoon dashi powder
- 1 pack (90–100 g/3¼–3½ oz) curry roux
- chilli (hot pepper) flakes, to taste

FOR THE STICKY OYSTER MUSHROOMS

- 1 tablespoon sesame oil
- 300 g (10½ oz) oyster mushrooms, roughly torn
- 3 tablespoons soy sauce
- 1 tablespoon sake
- 1 tablespoon light brown sugar
- 1 tablespoon sesame seeds

TO SERVE

- 4 portions ramen noodles
- a little vegetable oil
- curry powder or shichimi, to taste
- 1 sheet nori, cut into 8 pieces (optional)
- 4 eggs, medium-boiled and peeled (optional)
- a handful of bean sprouts, blanched (optional)
- a few spoonfuls of tinned corn (optional)
- a handful of coriander (cilantro), roughly chopped

METHOD

Slice about 2 inches' worth of the white part of the leek into rings as thinly as you can – use a sharp sharp knife and take your time. Place the shredded leek rings into a bowl of cold water and place in the refrigerator while you prepare the rest of the dish. Dice the rest of the leek.

Heat the chilli oil in a saucepan over a medium heat. Add the diced leek and the miso and stir them through the oil. Cook for about 5–6 minutes until they are browned. Add the tahini and stir through, then add the water and dashi powder and bring to the boil. Stir in the curry roux until it dissolves, then taste and adjust the seasoning as you like with chilli flakes.

Combine the sesame oil and mushrooms in a wok or large frying pan and set over a medium-high heat. Stir-fry the mushrooms until they have lost most of their moisture, browned and shrunk significantly, around 10 minutes. When the mushrooms are very dry and starting to catch on the pan, add the soy sauce, sake and sugar and continue to cook, stirring often, until the liquid evaporates once again and the mushrooms are dark and jammy. Stir in the sesame seeds, then remove from the heat.

Cook the ramen according to the package instructions, but a touch softer than you usually would – you'll be chilling them down and they won't be sitting in broth, so they'll remain quite firm. Drain the noodles and rinse them very well with plenty of cold water, to stop the cooking and remove excess starch. Toss the noodles with some vegetable oil to keep them from sticking together.

Divide the noodles between four serving plates and garnish with the curry powder or shichimi, nori, eggs, bean sprouts and corn (if using). Drain the chilled shredded leek well. Divide the hot curry soup between small bowls along with the mushrooms, and garnish with more chilli oil, the shredded leek and coriander. To eat, dip and swirl the noodles into the hot broth and slurp them up, along with the toppings, as you go.

SWEET & SPICY CURRY WINGS ✯

SERVES 2–4 AS A MAIN, OR UP TO 8 AS A SNACK

Curry roux is awesome not only for its flavour but also for it's thickening capabilities. This means it makes excellent clingy sauces. I especially like it on these wings, which have izakaya-meets-sports-bar vibes. You'll need napkins for your hands and straws for your beverages, because these will leave no fingertip unsullied.

INGREDIENTS

- 750 g (1 lb 10 oz) chicken wings, jointed
- 1 tablespoon baking powder
- salt and pepper
- 25 g (1 oz) curry roux
- 3 tablespoons Sriracha sauce or similar
- 2 tablespoons honey
- 1 tablespoon soy sauce
- juice of ½ lime
- sesame seeds and/or chilli (hot pepper) flakes, to garnish (optional)

METHOD

Preheat the oven to 200°C (400°F/gas 6).

Pat the wings dry with paper towels – get them really dry. Toss them with the baking powder and a sprinkle of salt and pepper, then transfer them to a baking tray fitted with a wire rack, laid out in a single layer. Bake for 40 minutes, turning halfway through.

Meanwhile, finely grate the curry roux and stir it together with the Sriracha, honey, soy sauce and lime juice. When the wings are cooked, toss them with the sauce, then return to the baking tray (without the rack this time). Place them back in the oven for another 3–4 minutes to cook out the roux and thicken the sauce.

If you like, you can garnish these with sesame seeds or chilli flakes. Serve with beer or chu-hai.

Karē Oyakodon
カレー親子丼

CURRY OYAKODON ✮

SERVES 2

Why have one comfort food when you can have two? This is a combination of curry rice and oyakodon – chicken and egg rice bowl. It's curry, it's chicken, it's eggs, and it comes together in about 20 minutes. What's not to love?

INGREDIENTS

- 1 tablespoon vegetable oil
- 1 onion, thinly sliced
- 2 skinless and boneless chicken thighs, cut into bite-size chunks
- a little salt and pepper
- 240 ml (7¾ fl oz/scant 1 cup) dashi or water
- about ⅓ pack (30 g/1 oz) curry roux
- 4 eggs, loosely beaten
- 2 portions freshly cooked rice
- aonori, shichimi and/or soy sauce, to garnish

METHOD

Pour the oil into a frying pan for which you have a lid and set over a medium-high heat, add the onion and cook until softened slightly. Add the chicken thighs and season everything with salt and pepper. Sauté for about 8 minutes until the chicken is just about cooked through and the onions have browned a bit. Add the dashi or water and bring to a simmer, then crumble in the curry roux and stir to dissolve.

Bring the curry sauce to the boil, then pour in the beaten eggs. Stir briefly, then place a lid on the pan and cook for another 3–4 minutes, stirring once again halfway through cooking. The eggs should still be very loose at the end.

Have some hot rice ready in deep bowls, then pile the curry egg mixture on top. Garnish with aonori, shichimi and/or soy sauce, as you see fit.

ラムネ

CHAPTER 9

お茶・飲み物

TEA & OTHER BEVERAGES

Like yuzu and miso, MATCHA (抹茶) is another one of those singular Japanese flavours that has recently taken the world by storm. It's an odd one, in a way. Matcha's flavour is intense and incomparable, and making it requires skill and special kit. Then again, the same could be said for espresso. I suppose we all contain multitudes; usually, I just want to nurse a cup of mellow diner coffee all day long, but sometimes I need the sensory pistol-whip of an oily doppio to feel alive. Such is matcha.

Traditionally, matcha was (and still is) profoundly connected to a particular mode of restrained, meditative Japanese aesthetics in the school of 16th-century tea master Sen no Rikyū – and now it's something we put in cheesecake and Frappuccinos. And that's fine! I love things that can go highbrow and lowbrow like that. It speaks to matcha's intriguing, irresistible flavour: bright, bitter and bracing, which can lift mellow flavours like vanilla, azuki and chocolate; or underscore tart ones like strawberries and citrus. It can even be used to season savoury dishes – mixed with salt, it's a perfect partner for fried food, like tempura.

Shopping for matcha can be annoying, because the low-grade stuff at one end of the spectrum can be utterly terrible, really astringent and dull in colour. But on the other end of the spectrum, it gets very expensive very quickly. It's hard to find a decent one in the middle.

Once again, it's CLEARSPRING to the rescue: their matcha is very good without being ludicrously pricey; and a little bit goes a long way anyway. But if you want to indulge in a real treat, I recommend LALANI AND CO.'s 'Matcha Gold', a rare single-origin organic matcha from Kagoshima. They also do a very good and very affordabe lower-grade cooking matcha.

Matcha is just one of dozens of delightful teas from Japan, and I really encourage you to try them, because there's actually a matcha shortage developing due to international demand. This has resulted in long-standing matcha buyers being priced out of the market; what was once an affordable luxury is becoming something only the rich can afford. The shortage has been driven largely by social media; it seems the TikTok crowd just can't get enough of green desserts, as we've also seen with pandan and the infamous pistachio-filled 'Dubai chocolate' trend. Hopefully, the whole thing will blow over soon, as people flock to the next big green thing. In the meantime, it may be best to ease off the matcha a bit, to give Japan's matcha growers and buyers a break, and curtail spiralling price inflation. All of the matcha recipes in this book can be made with alternative teas – just whizz the leaves through a spice grinder to make a powder.

And there are so many wonderful alternatives! There is, of course, all manner of RYOKUCHA (緑茶), a catch-all for green tea, including SENCHA (煎茶), which denotes whole-leaf tea, and KUKICHA (茎茶), which contains twigs and stems. Then there are specially processed teas, like Japanese versions of OOLONG (ŪRON CHA / 烏龍茶) and BLACK TEA (WA KŌCHA / 和紅茶); GENMAICHA (玄米茶), which contains toasted rice for bulk and a nutty flavour; and HŌJICHA (焙じ茶), which is roasted to produce a sweet, mellow tea with notes of autumn leaves and toffee. These teas are less commonly used in cooking than matcha, but that's mainly because they aren't usually sold as powders.

For the purposes of this book, there is one other 'tea' to talk about, which is MUGICHA (麦茶). This isn't actually tea, but an infusion made from dark-roasted barley. It is usually cold-infused and sold in large-format tea bags to be plunked into big jugs of water. Its flavour is lightly nutty and very refreshing.

There are a million other 'other beverages' produced in Japan – whiskey, shōchū, sake, amazake, chū-hai, hirezake, doburoku, awamori, beer, wine, Boss coffee, genki drinks, yuzu-shu, Calpis, melon soda, melon milk, etc. – but there are only two more I need to explain here: RAMUNE (ラムネ) and UMESHU (梅酒).

Ramune is Japanese lemonade, packaged in an iconic marble-sealed bottle. You can now get this everywhere, and in many flavours. But for me, and for the recipes in this book, it's got to be the original, which has a unique 7Up-bubble gum-Irn Bru flavour. Nothing tastes like summer more than regular ramune.

Umeshu, which is sometimes called 'plum wine', is actually a liqueur made from strong distilled alcohol, Japanese plums (*ume*) and lots of sugar. The best stuff has a heady aroma and a nice tartness to balance its syrupy sweetness. For cooking, any old plonk, like CHOYA or TAKARA, will be fine. For drinking, seek out UMESHUYA, the UK's only specialist umeshu importer. They have an outstanding selection, ranging from light and delicate to jammy and full-bodied.

Just like Japanese food, Japanese drinks reward curiosity. Start with the basics and an open mind, shop around, ask questions, and they will lead you down all sorts of fascinating, delicious paths. That's pretty much what I did when I was a kid – it all started with soy sauce and instant noodles ... and here I am. It is not an exaggeration to say that Japanese ingredients have influenced the trajectory of my whole life. Maybe they won't have quite that much of an impact on you – but at the very least, they'll have a big impact on your cooking.

Bīgan Matcha Chīzukēki
ビーガン抹茶チーズケーキ

VEGAN MATCHA-MISO DOUBLE CHEESECAKE ☆ ❦

SERVES 8

This vegan dessert is roughly inspired by the famous 'double fromage' cheesecake from Hokkaido's Le Tao bakery, which features a rich baked layer beneath a silky whipped layer. This version uses a generous quantity of matcha in the baked layer and a touch of miso in the top one, to replicate some of the tang of cream cheese. The fundamentals for this recipe came from Philip Khoury's *A New Way to Bake*, which is an outstanding resource if you're looking to de-animalise your baking.

INGREDIENTS

FOR THE CRUST

- 50 g (1¾ oz/3½ tablespoons) plant-based butter, melted, plus extra for greasing
- 200 g (7 oz) digestive biscuits (graham crackers)
- 25 g (1 oz/2 tablespoons) sugar
- a pinch of sea salt

FOR THE BAKED LAYER

- 350 g (12 oz) firm silken tofu
- juice of ½ lemon
- 70 g (2½ oz/scant ⅓ cup) sugar
- 20 g (¾ oz/1 tablespoon) maple syrup
- 2 tablespoons matcha
- 2 tablespoons olive oil
- 25 g (1 oz/scant ¼ cup) cornflour (cornstarch)
- 10 g (½ oz/3½ tablespoons) plain (all-purpose) flour

FOR THE WHIPPED LAYER

- 150 g (5½ oz) firm silken tofu
- 150 ml (5 fl oz/scant ⅔ cup) plant-based whipping cream
- 90 g (3¼ oz/¾ cup) icing (powdered) sugar
- 10 g (½ oz/2 teaspoons) smooth white miso
- 1 tablespoon vanilla bean paste
- 30 g (1 oz/2 tablespoons) plant-based butter or coconut oil, melted and cooled slightly
- 4 strawberries, halved, to decorate

METHOD

For the crust, line the base of a 23 cm (9 in) springform cake tin (pan) with baking paper and lightly grease it with plant-based butter.

Blitz the biscuits in a food processor to make a fine crumb, then pour in the plant-based butter and sugar and process until well mixed. Stir in the salt, then spread this mixture out in the lined tin, packing it down firmly in an even layer with your hands.

Preheat the oven to 150°C (300°F/gas 2).

Blitz all of the ingredients for the baked layer together in a food processor until smooth (there will be some tiny flecks of unblended tofu – that's fine). Scoop the filling mixture onto the biscuit base and spread it out evenly across the tin. Transfer to the oven and bake for 20 minutes. Allow to cool, then transfer to the refrigerator to chill completely.

For the whipped layer, combine all the ingredients except the plant-based butter (or oil) and strawberries in a large bowl and whip with an electric beater until thick and fluffy, somewhere between the texture of a custard and a mousse – this will take several minutes. Pour in the melted plant-based butter, a little at a time, as you continue to whip, to distribute it evenly throughout the mixture before it solidifies. The finished mixture will be glossy and smooth and still semi-liquid. Pour the whipped tofu cream on top of the cooled matcha layer, then transfer to the refrigerator to chill overnight.

Serve cold and decorate each slice with half a strawberry.

Matcha to Hōjicha to Genmaicha no Pafe
抹茶とほうじ茶と玄米茶のパフェ

TRIPLE TEA PARFAIT ✯

SERVES 4

This elaborate parfait requires a bit of effort in terms of prep, but your reward is a sensory adventure through the world of Japanese tea: hōjicha sponge cake, genmaicha ice cream and matcha syrup. Now, I'm not much for entertaining – I like having people around, but I'm not a 'nice cutlery' kind of person – but I do enjoy serving a dessert that gets a few *oohs* and *aahs*. This is that dessert.

INGREDIENTS

FOR THE GENMAICHA-COCONUT ICE CREAM

- 1 heaped tablespoon genmaicha
- 250 ml (8 fl oz/1 cup) whipping cream
- 1 x 210 g (7 oz) tin sweetened condensed coconut milk
- 1 tablespoon vanilla extract

FOR THE MATCHA-HONEY SYRUP

- 1 tablespoon hot (tap) water
- 1 teaspoon matcha
- 4 tablespoons honey

FOR THE HŌJICHA MICROWAVE SPONGE

- 1 heaped tablespoon hōjicha leaves
- 100 g (3½ oz/¾ cup) plain (all-purpose) flour
- 1 teaspoon baking powder
- a pinch of salt
- 100 ml (3½ fl oz/scant ½ cup) milk
- 100 g (3½ oz/½ cup) light brown sugar
- 2 tablespoons vegetable oil

TO SERVE

- whipped cream
- cherries or berries (fresh or frozen)
- strawberries (fresh or frozen)
- mango (fresh or frozen)
- various wafers and biscuits and whatnot

MAKE IT VEGAN

Use plant-based milk and whipping cream, and agave syrup instead of honey.

METHOD

To make the ice cream, place the genmaicha in a spice grinder and blitz to a fine powder. Pass the powder through a small sieve (fine mesh strainer), then stir it together with the remaining ingredients in a large mixing bowl. Beat with an electric whisk until thick and stiff, similar in texture to Greek yoghurt (be careful not to overbeat, or the cream may split). Transfer to a container, cover and freeze overnight, or until completely set.

To make the syrup, combine the hot water and matcha in a little jar and shake hard for about 30 seconds. Add the honey and stir well (or shake it again), then refrigerate until ready to use.

To make the sponge, grind the hōjicha to a fine powder in a spice grinder, then stir it together with the flour, baking powder and salt. Add the milk, sugar and oil and mix well, then place in a microwave-safe container, cover loosely and cook on full power (800W) for 3 minutes until steamed through. Leave to cool, then cut or tear the cake into chunks, a little smaller than bite-size.

To serve, simply layer the sponge pieces, ice cream and syrup in parfait glasses along with the whipped cream and fruit. Top with plenty of whipped cream and matcha syrup, along with a couple of wafers or biscuits.

Suika Umeshu Guranite
スイカ梅酒グラニテ

WATERMELON UMESHU GRANITA ✭ ❦

SERVES 4–8

Watermelon and umeshu are a power couple of frozen refreshment. This boozy granita is halfway between a cocktail and a sorbet and can be enjoyed as either.

INGREDIENTS

- 500 g (1 lb 2 oz) watermelon (prepared weight), deseeded
- 100 ml (3½ fl oz/scant ½ cup) umeshu, plus extra to serve
- lemon or lime juice, to taste
- crushed sea salt flakes, to garnish

METHOD

Blend the watermelon and umeshu together to a smooth purée, then taste. If you want it to have a little more zip, add a touch of lemon or lime juice (this will depend on how sour the umeshu is, and if you want it to be tart at all).

Transfer to the freezer. Stir the liquid from time to time and break up any frozen chunks as it freezes, which will make it easier to serve later. When it's completely frozen, scrape with a fork to create a light, snowy texture.

Serve in little glasses, perhaps with more chilled umeshu poured on top. Garnish with a tiny bit of sea salt just before serving.

梅酒

MATCHA MIDORI GRASSHOPPER

MAKES 1 COCKTAIL, BUT SERVES AT LEAST 2 (YOU'LL SEE WHAT I MEAN)

I was surprised to learn in researching this recipe that Midori – the famous green melon liqueur for children – is Japanese. I always assumed it wasn't, because of its unimaginative Japanese name ('midori' just means 'green') and because it isn't that common at bars in Japan. But it is, in fact, a Suntory product, invented in 1964. It makes sense that it was invented in Japan, as melon-flavoured drinks have been popular there for decades, and the flavour works surprisingly well with another green M: matcha. This recipe makes it a hat-trick, adding mint in the form of créme de menthe to create a twist on the classic retro cocktail known as a Grasshopper. At the Hob Nob restaurant in my hometown, the 'drink' is made with so much ice cream it can be piled into a Matterhorn-like peak that rises high above the rim of the glass. Is it a cocktail? Or some kind of absurd sundae? I say: why not both?

INGREDIENTS

- 6 tablespoons Midori (green melon liqueur)
- 2 tablespoons crème de menthe, plus a little more to drizzle
- 1 tablespoon matcha, plus extra for sprinkling
- 300 g (10½ oz) ice cubes
- 475 g (1 lb 1 oz/2 cups) vanilla ice cream
- 1 Maraschino cherry

METHOD

Combine the liqueurs and matcha in a blender and whizz them on low speed to disperse the matcha. Add the ice and blend until it forms a dense slush, then add the ice cream and blend until smooth and well mixed. It will be very thick – you have this with a spoon, not a straw, so resist the urge to add liquid, if it's hard to blend. Just let it sit for a few minutes and the ice cream will soften, at which point you can blend again.

Scoop the cocktail out into a comically large cocktail glass or ice cream coupe, piling it up as you go. Decorate with a little sprinkle of matcha, a drizzle of crème de menthe and a cherry on top.

MAKE IT VEGAN

Many tasty plant-based vanilla ice creams exist these days, and they will work splendidly!

MAPLE MUGICHA HIGHBALL

SERVES 1

I don't drink much anymore, but sometimes I still crave a particular cocktail that I've been drinking since college: the simple, classic whisky highball. This non-alcoholic version approximates its flavour using the roasty-toasty flavour of mugicha with a touch of woody sweetness from maple syrup – but it's still dry, as I like it.

INGREDIENTS

- 1–2 mugicha tea bags
- 3 shots (75 ml/2½ fl oz/5 tablespoons) strong mugicha (see method)
- 1–1½ teaspoons maple syrup (depending on whether you want it sweeter or drier)
- 1 teaspoon lemon juice
- 100 ml (3½ fl oz/scant ½ cup) soda water
- ice cubes
- a splash of ginger ale or beer (optional)
- 1 wheel of lemon, to garnish (optional)

METHOD

Most mugicha comes in tea bags which are designed to infuse into 1 litre (34 fl oz/4¼ cups) cold water for about 1 hour. To make a stronger one, just double the ratio – use 2 bags per litre, or 1 bag per 500 ml (17 fl oz/2 cups). You can also speed up the process, and make an even stronger brew, by using hot water and then chilling it down.

Combine the mugicha, maple syrup and lemon juice in a highball glass and stir well. Add a splash of soda water to thin it out, then fill the glass with ice and top up with soda water, finishing with a splash of ginger beer (if you like). Stir well and garnish with lemon.

Ramune no Kakuteru no Mittsu
ラムネのカクテルの３つ

THREE RAMUNE COCKTAILS

ALL SERVE 1

On a hot summer day, there's nothing I'd rather drink than an ice-cold ramune – except maybe a delicious cocktail made from ramune. These are just a few suggestions – ramune also takes well to vodka, gin, Scotch, tequila, rum ... just about anything you have in your cabinet.

RAMUNE AND RYE

The ramune highball is where the ridiculous meets the sublime: the bubblegum childhood sweetness of Japanese lemonade combined with the cigarette-stained salaryman despair of whiskey or shochu. But that's why it works – it's a nostalgia-soaked midlife crisis in a glass!

INGREDIENTS

- ice, as needed
- 1–2 shots (25–50 ml/1–1¾ fl oz/scant 3–3½ tablespoons) rye whiskey (or any whiskey, really)
- about 2 teaspoons lemon, lime or yuzu juice
- 100–125 ml (3½–4 fl oz/scant ½–½ cup) ramune
- 1 wheel of lemon and/or a Maraschino cherry, to garnish (both optional)

METHOD

Fill a Collins glass or tumbler with ice and pour in the whiskey and lemon juice. Top up with ramune and stir. Garnish with lemon and/or a cherry.

RAMUNE RADLER

The child in me associates summertime with ramune; the old man in me associates it with cold lager. Here we have the best of both worlds, for the ultimate summertime refresher.

INGREDIENTS

- 200 ml (7 fl oz/scant 1 cup) ramune
- 200 ml (7 fl oz/scant 1 cup) lager (bland is good here – Japanese lagers work well)
- a dash of grapefruit juice, yuzu juice and/or a squeeze of lemon (optional)
- ice, as needed

METHOD

Pour the ramune and lager into a pint glass along with the citrus juice (if using). Add enough ice to raise the liquid to the top of the glass. Drink in the sunshine.

DIMPLES

This candy-sweet kiddy cocktail's name is a reference to the little indents on a ramune bottle that keep the marble from slipping back down into the bottleneck, and to the 1936 film starring Shirley Temple, whose namesake drink inspired this one.

INGREDIENTS

- 100 ml (3½ fl oz/scant ½ cup) ramune
- 1 tablespoon pineapple juice
- 1 tablespoon grapefruit or orange juice
- ice, as needed
- 1 tablespoon grenadine
- prepared fruit, such as orange, lime, pineapple, grapes, etc., to garnish
- 1 Maraschino cherry, to garnish

METHOD

Pour the ramune and juices into a tumbler and add ice to fill. Stir gently, then top with the grenadine. Skewer the fruit and the cherry onto a cocktail stick and set on top of the drink.

KIMURA
RAMUNE
元祖
ラムネ
ORIGINAL FLAVOUR

CHAPTER 10

タレの図書館

THE LIBRARY OF CONDIMENTS

A lot of Japanese home cooking is about having an arsenal of delicious sauces, marinades and condiments at your disposal. These condiments are based on the same storecupboard staples around which this book is structured, combined in ways that make them even more than the sum of their parts. They're a great way to elevate humble ingredients, and they have an exceptionally high effort-to-deliciousness ratio.

What follows are 40 recipes – mostly traditional, but a few of my own invention – divided into four categories: dips and dressings, marinades and brines, glazes and sauces, and soup and noodle seasonings. Many of these can fall into more than one of these categories depending on how they're used, but for the sake of simplicity I've limited them to the one they're most commonly used for. To navigate this list, I've arranged them on an axis ranging from KIKI to BOUBA.

Allow me to explain. The 'bouba/kiki effect' is an example of synaesthetic associations between sounds and shapes. We think of soft, rounded shapes when we hear the word 'bouba', and sharp, angular ones when we hear the word 'kiki' (and vice versa: we think of softer sounds when we see curvy shapes, and more percussive ones when we see pointy shapes).

The effect was first observed in 1924 and has been confirmed in dozens of studies since then. It is considered to be universal, occurring across cultures and languages. (It is worth noting that although the words easily map to Japanese phonemes, they are not Japanese words. They're nonsense words made up by an American scientist.)

'KIKI' ON THE LEFT, 'BOUBA' ON THE RIGHT.

I first heard about this phenomenon when Heston Blumenthal wrote about it years ago, pointing out that the association applies to flavour, as well. Kiki flavours are sharp, acidic, spicy and salty; bouba ones are rich, umami and sweet. As you may expect, the sounds have a textural association, too. Kiki textures are crisp, brittle and crunchy; bouba textures are creamy, soft, chewy and sticky. For our purposes, kiki sauces also tend to be thinner, while bouba ones are more viscous.

Basically, kiki and bouba are useful shorthands for understanding the overall flavour profile of each of these sauces, and also what they bring to a meal in terms of balance. For example, if you're serving a rich, bouba cut of braised meat, you might want a kiki-fresh salad or some kiki-sour pickles for contrast. The classic Japanese meal format of rice, miso soup and pickles is actually a perfect example of kiki-bouba balance in action; a zingy umeboshi (pickled plum) provides the perfect contrast to the mellow starchiness of the rice and round umami of the soup.

There are a lot of recipes here, so thinking in terms of balance and working backwards like this can help you figure out where to begin. When in doubt, look for the star! ☆ These are my favourites.

KIKI

DIPS & DRESSINGS	MARINADES & BRINES	GLAZES & PAN SAUCES	SOUP SEASONINGS & NOODLE SAUCES
SCOTCH BONNET HONEY PONZU ★ (P.190)			
SALTED PONZU (P.191)			
PONZU, TWO WAYS ★ (P.193)	RICE VINEGAR PICKLE BRINE (P.203)		
CARROT & GINGER DRESSING (P.193)	SUSHI VINEGAR (P.203)		
	SOUR PLUM MISO ★ (P.205)		
	SOY SAUCE PICKLE BRINE (P.205)		
SHICHIMI, SANSHŌ & SATSUMA CHILLI OIL (P.197)			
VINEGARED MISO (P.198)			
MISO MUSTARD ★ (P.198)		GINGER STIR-FRY SAUCE (P.207)	
		JAPANESE BARBECUE SAUCE (P.207)	
YUZU GINGER MISO DRESSING ★ (P.194)	YUZU MISO (P.206)		VEGAN BROCCOLI MISO PESTO ★ (P.213)
SOUR PLUM & SHISO DRESSING ★ (P.194)			
NOT-THAT-SPICY CHILLI CRISP ★ (P.197)			
GYOZA DIP (P.199)	DASHI VINEGAR (P.204)		
SWEET ONION & GINGER DRESSING ★ (P.191)	SWEETENED SOY SAUCE VINEGAR (P.204)		YAKISOBA SAUCE (P.214)
			THICK AND GLOSSY DASHI SAUCE (P.214)
		EEL SAUCE ★ (P.209)	
WASABI & PICKLED GINGER TARTARE SAUCE ★ (P.200)		YAKITORI SAUCE (P.209)	
SALTED LEEK RELISH (P.199)			
JAPANESE TARTARE SAUCE (P.200)		GARLIC GINGER MISO BUTTER (P.212)	SUKIYAKI SAUCE ★ (P.215)
		TWO-INGREDIENT TERIYAKI (P.210)	SOY SAUCE SEASONING FOR NOODLES (P.215)
		HONEY MISO (P.210)	GARLIC MISO SESAME DRESSING ★ (P.216)
VEGAN JAPANESE MAYO (P.201)		SOY SAUCE BUTTER ★ (P.212)	NOODLE SOUP BROTH CONCENTRATE ★ (P.216)
SESAME MAYO (P.201)			MISO-MOCHI VEGAN 'CHEESE' SAUCE ★ (P.213)

BOUBA

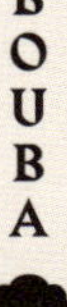

Shōga Ninjin Doresshingu 生姜人参ドレッシング

CARROT & GINGER DRESSING

MAKES ABOUT 350 ML (12 FL OZ/1½ CUPS), ENOUGH FOR AT LEAST 6 SERVINGS

USE For crisp, leafy salads or slaws.

TASTES Healthy! Sweet, gingery, sharp and invigorating.

INGREDIENTS

- 1 medium carrot, peeled and roughly chopped
- 1 cm (½ in) thick slice of fresh root ginger, peeled
- 4 tablespoons white miso or soy sauce
- 4 tablespoons water
- 4 tablespoons mirin
- 4 tablespoons rice vinegar
- 2 tablespoons olive oil or sesame oil

METHOD

Combine all the ingredients in a blender and purée until as smooth as you can get it.

Store in a jar in the refrigerator for up to 1 month, and shake well each time you use it.

Wafū Doresshingu 和風ドレッシング

SWEET ONION & GINGER DRESSING ☆

MAKES ABOUT 350 ML (12 FL OZ/1½ CUPS), ENOUGH FOR AT LEAST 6 SERVINGS

USE On all sorts of salads, including warm roasted veg ones. Great with steak, too.

TASTES Sharp, deeply savoury, oniony, gingery and very wafū.

INGREDIENTS

- ¼ small onion or ½ banana shallot
- 2 cm (¾ in) piece of fresh root ginger, peeled
- 100 ml (3½ fl oz/scant ½ cup) soy sauce
- 100 ml (3½ fl oz/scant ½ cup) rice vinegar
- 4 tablespoons mirin
- 2 tablespoons sugar (light brown works well)
- 1 tablespoon oil (vegetable, olive or sesame all work)
- 1 tablespoon sesame seeds
- ½ teaspoon dashi powder (optional)

METHOD

Combine everything in a blender and purée until the onion and ginger are broken down and the sugar is dissolved.

Store in a jar in the refrigerator for up to 6 months, and shake well before each use.

MAKE IT VEGAN

Use kombu dashi powder.

SCOTCH BONNET HONEY PONZU ✯

MAKES ABOUT 200 ML (7 FL OZ/SCANT 1 CUP)

USE Anywhere you'd want sweet chilli sauce, but with a LOT more punch. It is exceptional on fried chicken.

TASTES Extremely spicy and citrussy, barely reined in by honey sweetness.

INGREDIENTS

- 4 tablespoons water
- 3 tablespoons soy sauce
- 30 g (1 oz/2 tablespoons) sugar
- 30 g (1 oz/4 teaspoons) honey
- 1 teaspoon fine salt
- ½ teaspoon kombu dashi powder or MSG
- 2 fresh Scotch bonnet chillies, destemmed and chopped
- 1 garlic clove, peeled
- 4 tablespoons sour citrus juice (yuzu, lemon, lime, etc.)

METHOD

Combine everything except the citrus juice in a small saucepan and bring to the boil. Reduce to a simmer and cook for about 5 minutes to soften the chillies, then remove from the heat and blend until smooth. Stir in the citrus juice and leave to cool.

This lasts indefinitely in the refrigerator, and in fact tastes better after a month or two.

Shio Ponzu 塩ポン酢

SALTED PONZU

MAKES ABOUT 200 ML (7 FL OZ/SCANT 1 CUP)

USE Wherever a lighter, more citrussy ponzu flavour is preferred. It is a good curing medium for ceviche (page 143), and also amazing on oysters.

TASTES Like pure salty citrus freshness, with a little sweetness and umami.

INGREDIENTS

- 100 ml (3½ fl oz/scant ½ cup) warm water
- a small piece of kombu (about 2.5 x 5 cm/1 x 2 in)
- 4 tablespoons sour citrus juice (yuzu, lemon, lime, etc.)
- 2 tablespoons mirin
- 2 tablespoons sugar
- 1 tablespoon rice vinegar
- 15 g (½ oz/1 tablespoon) salt

METHOD

Combine all the ingredients and stir to dissolve the salt and sugar. Leave for at least an hour to infuse the kombu before using.

Store in the refrigerator for up to 6 months.

Ponzu no Tsukurikata Futatsu ポン酢の作り方２つ

PONZU, TWO WAYS ✯

USE On everything! Especially sashimi, chicken, noodles and dumplings. Add a little oil to make a versatile vinaigrette.

TASTES Sour with citrus, savoury with soy sauce. One of my all-time favourites.

NOTE I have provided no specific quantities here, so you can make as much as you like based on how much juice you get from the fresh citrus fruit you have. I recommend making a big batch when citrus is in season to last you through the year. You can choose any citrus fruits you like, provided that the overall impact is tart. This year, I used a mix of bergamot, lime, yuzu, grapefruit and satsuma, and it was my best ponzu ever.

The ratios in these methods refer to volume rather than weight. You will need a microplane grater and, ideally, a citrus squeezer (not a reamer) for this, so you can extract plenty of essential oils, which are key to an aromatic and zingy ponzu.

INGREDIENTS

THE 5-4-3-2-1 METHOD

- finely grated zest of all your citrus
- 5 parts shōyu
- 4 parts tart citrus juice
- 3 parts mirin
- 2 parts dashi (from a powder is fine) or sake
- 1 part vinegar
- sugar (optional, to taste)

THE 50/50 METHOD

- finely grated zest of all your citrus
- 1 part shōyu
- 1 part tart citrus juice
- salt and sugar, as needed, to taste

FOR BOTH METHODS

Before juicing your citrus, zest them all with a fine microplane, being careful to avoid the pith. Combine the zest with the shōyu in a saucepan and bring to a bare simmer over a medium heat, then leave to infuse as it cools.

FOR THE 5-4-3-2-1 METHOD

Stir all of the remaining ingredients into the infused soy sauce, then pass through a sieve (fine mesh strainer), pressing down on the zest with a spoon or spatula to extract as much oil as possible. Taste the sauce; if it is too aggressively sour, add a little sugar to balance it.

FOR THE 50/50 METHOD

Stir the citrus juice into the infused soy sauce, then pass through a sieve (fine mesh strainer), pressing down on the zest with a spoon or spatula to extract as much oil as possible. Taste the sauce; if it is too aggressively sour, add a little sugar to balance it.

You may also need to add a bit of salt to help preserve the juice, but this will depend on the soy sauce you've used. Usukuchi soy sauces will already be salty enough, but if you've used an all-purpose shōyu or tamari, stir in a bit of salt until the ponzu tastes noticeably salty – not quite as salty as soy sauce itself, but almost.

Both versions can be transferred to to a clean bottle or jar and kept in the refrigerator for up to a year.

Yuzu Shōga Miso Doresshingu
柚子生姜味噌ドレッシング

YUZU GINGER MISO DRESSING ✯ ❦

MAKES ABOUT 350 ML (12 FL OZ/1½ CUPS), ENOUGH FOR AT LEAST 6 SERVINGS

USE For salads, but also as a marinade for pork or chicken, or a sauce for oily fish.

TASTES Extremely zingy and aromatic, and a bit spicy from the ginger.

INGREDIENTS

- 3 cm (1¼ in) thick slice of fresh root ginger, peeled and thinly sliced against the grain
- 4 tablespoons white miso
- 4 tablespoons water
- 4 tablespoons mirin
- 4 tablespoons yuzu juice
- 2 tablespoons olive oil
- ¼ teaspoon MSG or kombu dashi powder

METHOD

Combine all the ingredients in a blender and purée until as smooth as you can get it.

Store in a jar in the refrigerator for up to 1 month and shake well each time you use it.

MAKE IT VEGAN

Use kombu dashi powder.

Ume-shiso Doresshingu
梅しそドレッシング

SOUR PLUM & SHISO DRESSING ✯ ❦

MAKES 250 ML (8 FL OZ/1 CUP), ENOUGH FOR ABOUT 6 SALADS

USE As a salad dressing (possibly the best salad dressing ever), or as a marinade for chicken or pork.

TASTES Sweet, sour and delightfully fragrant with shiso and umeboshi.

NOTE Shiso is a Japanese herb with a fresh, peppery flavour, which tastes a bit like a combination of mint and basil. You do not need fresh shiso for this recipe (which is hard to get), but you do need Yukari, a popular brand of purple shiso furikake (rice seasoning).

INGREDIENTS

- 6 tablespoons soy sauce
- 6 tablespoons rice vinegar
- 1 umeboshi (pickled plum), stoned and finely chopped
- 4 tablespoons mirin
- 2 tablespoons sugar
- 1 tablespoon olive or vegetable oil
- 1 tablespoon Yukari (shiso furikake)
- ¼–½ teaspoon dashi powder (optional – katsuo is preferable but kombu is fine too)

METHOD

Combine everything in a jar and shake until the sugar is dissolved, or just whisk everything together in a bowl.

Store in a jar in the refrigerator for up to 6 months, and shake well before each use.

SHICHIMI, SANSHŌ & SATSUMA CHILLI OIL

MAKES ABOUT 250 ML (8 FL OZ/1 CUP)

USE On dumplings, ramen or anything that needs a kick and an aroma boost.

TASTES Pretty spicy, with an intriguing orange aroma and a slight buzz from the sanshō.

INGREDIENTS

- ½ satsuma
- 200 ml (7 fl oz/scant 1 cup) vegetable oil
- 50 g (1¾ oz) fresh root ginger, peeled and finely diced
- 1 banana shallot, finely diced
- 3 tablespoons chilli (hot pepper) flakes
- 2 tablespoons soy sauce
- 1 tablespoon shichimi
- 1 tablespoon sanshō
- 1 tablespoon each black and white sesame seeds, coarsely crushed
- 1 teaspoon ground ginger
- 4 tablespoons sesame oil
- 3 tablespoons aonori (optional)

METHOD

Grate or finely chop the satsuma peel; reserve the segments.

Combine the oil, fresh ginger, shallot and satsuma peel in a small saucepan and set over a medium-low heat. Cook slowly, stirring occasionally, to cook off their moisture before they darken. After about 10–15 minutes, they should be golden brown.

At this point, add the juice from the reserved satsuma segments, the chilli flakes and the soy sauce. Increase the heat to medium and cook for about 5 minutes, stirring frequently, until the sizzling subsides and the chilli flakes have darkened slightly.

Remove from heat and stir in the shichimi, sanshō, sesame seeds and ground ginger, then add the sesame oil and aonori (if using). Leave to cool before transferring to a clean jar.

This will keep in the refrigerator for several months.

'Karasō de Karakunai Sukoshi Karai Taberu Rāyu' Mitai na Rāyu
「辛そうで辛くない少し辛いラー油」みたいなラー油

NOT-THAT-SPICY CHILLI CRISP

MAKES ABOUT 150 ML (5 FL OZ/SCANT ⅔ CUP)

USE Where you want a good, flavourful chilli crisp, but not too much heat.

TASTES Garlicky, spicy, crunchy, oily and umami, with a touch of toffee sweetness.

INGREDIENTS

- 5 tablespoons sesame oil
- 5 tablespoons vegetable oil
- 1 banana shallot, very thinly sliced
- 6 garlic cloves, very thinly sliced
- 25 g (1 oz) almonds or similar sweet nuts or seeds, thinly sliced or finely chopped
- ¼ teaspoon salt
- ¼ teaspoon MSG
- 1 tablespoon chilli (hot pepper) flakes
- 1 teaspoon paprika (any kind – this is mostly for colour, but you can use hot paprika for more heat, or smoked for a smoky note)

METHOD

Combine the oils and the shallot in a saucepan and set over a medium-low heat. Cook for 7–8 minutes, stirring occasionally, until the shallots have softened and barely begun to colour. Add the garlic and nuts and continue to cook, stirring occasionally, until the garlic is blond in colour. Stir in the salt, MSG, chilli flakes and paprika, then remove from the heat. The garlic, shallots and nuts should be a rich bronze-orange colour in the end, but they'll continue to cook in the oil as it cools, so take the oil off the heat well before they darken. (You can always put this back on the heat to cook more, if you need to, but even slightly burnt garlic will ruin the oil.)

Leave to cool, then pour everything into a jar. Store at room temperature and stir well before each use.

Sumiso 酢味噌

VINEGARED MISO

MAKES ABOUT 6–8 SERVINGS AS A DIP

USE As a dressing for crunchy vegetables or strong-flavoured sashimi, like tuna or squid. It can also be used as a pickling medium.

TASTES Funky, salty, sour and a little sweet.

INGREDIENTS

- 4 tablespoons miso (white, mixed or barley)
- 2 tablespoons rice vinegar
- 2 tablespoons sugar

METHOD

Stir together all of the ingredients until no lumps remain. Store in the refrigerator for up to a year.

MISO MUSTARD ☆

MAKES 6 TABLESPOONS, ENOUGH FOR ABOUT 6–8 SERVINGS

USE Wherever one would ordinarily use a moderately strong mustard. Excellent with a smoky Polish sausage.

TASTES Like mustard! But with the fruity-umami twang of miso.

INGREDIENTS

- 4 tablespoons mustard (Dijon or grain mustard is my preference, but any will do)
- 2 tablespoons miso (white or mixed)

METHOD

Stir together both ingredients until no lumps remain. Store in the refrigerator for up to a year.

Negishio ねぎ塩

SALTED LEEK RELISH

MAKES 4 SERVINGS, OR ENOUGH TO MARINATE/SEASON 500 G (1 LB 2 OZ) MEAT

USE As a marinade or sauce for grilled meat, especially pork and lamb.

TASTES Salty, oniony, a little sweet and nutty with sesame oil.

INGREDIENTS

- ½ leek (the white part)
- 3 tablespoons sesame oil
- 1 tablespoon lemon juice
- 1 tablespoon soy sauce
- 1 tablespoon mirin
- 1 tablespoon sake
- 1 garlic clove, finely grated
- ½ teaspoon salt
- ½ teaspoon MSG or kombu dashi powder
- lots of black or white pepper, to taste

METHOD

Chop the leek very finely, then stir everything together. Alternatively, blitz everything together in a food processor until the leek is broken down into a coarse relish.

Keep in the refrigerator for up to a week. Marinate thinly sliced meat or chunks of chicken for up to a day before cooking.

Gyoza no Tare 餃子のタレ

GYOZA DIP

MAKES 2 SERVINGS SIMPLY SCALE UP AS NEEDED

USE As a dip for gyoza, or other rich and meaty dishes.

TASTES Salty and sharp.

INGREDIENTS

- 2 tablespoons soy sauce
- 1 tablespoon vinegar, ideally Chinese black vinegar
- a few drops of chilli oil or sesame oil

METHOD

Stir everything together and it's ready to go. You can also make this ahead of time and infuse it with a little bit of shredded fresh root ginger.

Tarutaru Sōsu タルタルソース

JAPANESE TARTARE SAUCE

MAKES ABOUT 120 ML (4 FL OZ/½ CUP), ENOUGH FOR 4 SERVINGS

USE Wherever you'd use tartare sauce – on fish or shellfish, but also sandwiches and fried chicken (see recipe, page 84).

TASTES Eggy, oniony, tangy and creamy.

INGREDIENTS

- 40 g (1½ oz) gherkins or cornichons
- 1 egg, hard-boiled, cooled, peeled and chopped
- ½ banana shallot or ¼ small onion, chopped
- 40 g (1½ oz) mayonnaise
- finely grated zest and juice of ¼ lemon (or 1 teaspoon lemon juice)
- ¼ teaspoon dried parsley or dill
- ¼ teaspoon Dijon, Japanese or English mustard
- a big pinch of MSG
- a grind of black pepper
- salt or celery salt, to taste

METHOD

Squeeze the pickles firmly to expel excess liquid from them, then chop them up. Stir everything together until well mixed. Store in the refrigerator for up to 5 days.

WASABI & PICKLED GINGER TARTARE SAUCE ✯ 🍃

MAKES ABOUT 100 ML (3½ FL OZ/SCANT ½ CUP), ENOUGH FOR UP TO 4 SERVINGS

USE For fried fish and shellfish, tempura vegetables or chunky chopped salads.

TASTES The way a sushi bar smells.

INGREDIENTS

- 20 g (¾ oz) pickled ginger (any kind), finely chopped
- 4 tablespoons mayonnaise or vegan mayonnaise
- 1 tablespoon wasabi
- 1 tablespoon aonori flakes or nori, cut into tiny bits
- 1 teaspoon lemon or yuzu juice
- 1 teaspoon soy sauce
- 1 teaspoon rice vinegar
- a few sprigs of dill, tarragon and/or flat-leaf parsley, chopped
- 1 spring onion (scallion) or a handful of chives, finely chopped

METHOD

Stir everything together until well mixed. Store in the refrigerator for up to a week.

Goma Mayo 胡麻マヨ

SESAME MAYO

MAKES ABOUT 120 ML (4 FL OZ/½ CUP), ENOUGH FOR UP TO 8 SMALL SALADS

USE As a rich, thick salad dressing – it is especially good with robust, crunchy veg like cabbage, carrots, radishes or parsnips.

TASTES Like mayonnaise, with the nutty richness of toasted sesame.

INGREDIENTS

- 3 tablespoons sesame seeds, toasted and ground to the consistency of coarse sand
- 60 g (2 oz) mayonnaise or vegan mayonnaise
- 2 tablespoons tahini
- 2 tablespoons soy sauce
- 1½ tablespoons sesame oil
- 1 tablespoon rice vinegar

METHOD

Stir everything together until well mixed. Keep in the fridge for up to a week.

VEGAN JAPANESE MAYO

MAKES ABOUT 300 ML (10 FL OZ/1¼ CUPS)

USE As a substitute for Kewpie when no Kewpie is to be found, or when you need a more dietary-inclusive version of Kewpie.

TASTES Just like Kewpie!

This recipe is adapted from *Vegan JapanEasy*.

INGREDIENTS

- 100 ml (3½ fl oz/scant ½ cup) unsweetened soy milk
- 200 ml (7 fl oz/scant 1 cup) neutral vegetable oil
- 1 tablespoon nutritional yeast flakes
- 1 tablespoon Dijon mustard
- 1 tablespoon rice vinegar
- ½ teaspoon soy sauce
- ½ teaspoon salt
- ¼ teaspoon MSG

METHOD

Blend everything in a blender until smooth and thick. Store in the refrigerator for up to 1 month.

Asazuke no Moto 浅漬けの素

RICE VINEGAR PICKLE BRINE

MAKES ABOUT 500 ML (17 FL OZ/2 CUPS),
ENOUGH TO MAKE 2–3 BIG JARS OF PICKLES

USE FOR Pickling any crunchy veg.

TASTES Sharp, a little sweet and very refreshing.

INGREDIENTS

- 100 ml (3½ fl oz/scant ½ cup) water
- 10 g (½ oz) kombu (or ½ teaspoon kombu dashi powder)
- 100 g (3½ oz/scant ½ cup) sugar
- 2 teaspoons salt
- 1 very small pinch chilli (hot pepper) flakes, a few shreds of citrus zest and/or a few slices of fresh root ginger (all optional)
- 400 ml (14 fl oz/generous 1½ cups) rice vinegar

METHOD

Combine the water, kombu, sugar, salt and chilli, zest or ginger (if using) in a saucepan and bring to a low simmer. Remove from the heat, stir to dissolve the sugar, and leave to infuse until the mixture cools.

Add the rice vinegar and transfer to a jar (don't pass it through a sieve/strainer – keep the kombu and everything in there). This will keep in the cupboard indefinitely and can be used to pickle any veg in a matter of hours; just pack your veg into a jar and pour over enough brine to cover.

Sushi-su 寿司酢

SUSHI VINEGAR

MAKES ABOUT 150 ML (5 FL OZ/SCANT ⅔ CUP),
ENOUGH FOR 2 BATCHES OF SUSHI RICE (FROM 300 G/10½ OZ UNCOOKED, TO MAKE ABOUT 32 PIECES OF SUSHI)

USE FOR Seasoning cooked rice for sushi, or to lightly dress vegetables.

TASTES Sharp, sweet and salty.

INGREDIENTS

- 150 ml (5 fl oz/scant ⅔ cup) rice vinegar
- 60 g (2 oz/generous ¼ cup) sugar
- 2 teaspoons fine salt
- 1 small piece of kombu (around 4 cm/1½ in square)

METHOD

Combine all of the ingredients in a saucepan and bring to a bare simmer, then stir to dissolve the sugar and salt. Leave to cool and infuse the kombu for at least 20 minutes.

For instructions on making sushi rice, see page 100.

Sanbaizu 三杯酢

SWEETENED SOY SAUCE VINEGAR

MAKES 150–180 ML (5–6 FL OZ/SCANT ⅔–¾ CUP), ENOUGH FOR 6 SERVINGS OF SUNOMONO OR 2 SMALL BATCHES OF PICKLES

USE FOR To dress sunomono or as a quick pickle brine. Also works as a dip for dumplings or fried food.

TASTES Equally umami, sweet and sour.

INGREDIENTS

- 4 tablespoons soy sauce
- 4 tablespoons rice vinegar
- 4 tablespoons sugar or mirin

METHOD

Stir everything together. If you're using sugar instead of mirin, you can bring the the liquid to a low boil dissolve it, but let it cool before using. This will keep for about 1 month in the refrigerator, but pickles made with this as a brine should be eaten within a week because it is not very salty or acidic.

Tosazu 土佐酢

DASHI VINEGAR

MAKES ABOUT 180 ML (6 FL OZ/¾ CUP), ENOUGH FOR 6 SERVINGS OF SUNOMONO OR 2 SMALL BATCHES OF PICKLES

USE FOR To dress sunomono and salads, or as a light pickle brine.

TASTES Bright and acidic, but with the smoky umami of katsuo.

INGREDIENTS

- 6 tablespoons rice vinegar
- 4 tablespoons Katsuo Dashi (page 23)
- 2 tablespoons soy sauce
- 1 tablespoon mirin or sugar

METHOD

Stir everything together. If you're using sugar instead of mirin, you can bring the the liquid to a low boil to dissolve it, but let it cool before using. This will keep for about 1 month in the refrigerator, but pickles made with this as a brine should be eaten within a week because it is not very salty or acidic.

Shōyuzuke no Moto 醤油漬けの素

SOY SAUCE PICKLE BRINE

MAKES ABOUT 250 ML (8 FL OZ/1 CUP), ENOUGH FOR 2–3 SMALL JARS OF PICKLES

USE For making sweet-salty pickles. It also makes a pretty good dip for fatty/meaty foods, like gyoza or salmon tataki.

TASTES Salty, umami, sweet and sour.

INGREDIENTS

- 200 ml (7 fl oz/scant 1 cup) soy sauce
- 80 g (2¾ oz/⅓ cup) sugar
- 3 tablespoons rice vinegar
- chilli (hot pepper) flakes, to taste
- 1 garlic clove, smashed (optional)
- salt, as needed

METHOD

Combine the soy sauce, sugar, vinegar, chilli and garlic in a saucepan and bring to a bare simmer. Stir to dissolve the sugar, then set aside to cool.

Prepare any vegetables you like by salting them heavily to draw out their water for 30 minutes, then rinse them well and squeeze firmly to expel excess liquid. Pack the prepared vegetables into sterilised containers and pour over the brine. Leave to pickle overnight, or for up to a week.

Umeboshi Miso 梅干し味噌

SOUR PLUM MISO ☆

MAKES ABOUT 150 ML (5 FL OZ/SCANT ⅔ CUP), ENOUGH FOR ABOUT 6–8 SERVINGS AS A MARINADE OR DIP

USE As a punchy dip or pickling medium for raw vegetables; a topping for rice; or a marinade for chicken, duck or pork. Also great with mature cheese.

TASTES Quite sour and salty with a slight sweetness and deep umami.

Traditional recipes for ume-miso use tart green Japanese ume plums steeped in sugar and miso over several weeks before blending. As these are not readily available, this recipe approximates the flavour using fresh and pickled plums instead. The fresh plum can be ripe or unripe, but if you use unripe, you may want to add more sugar.

INGREDIENTS

- 1 fresh plum (or ½ nectarine), stoned and chopped
- 4 umeboshi (pickled plums), stoned
- 4 tablespoons red miso (or better yet, moromi miso)
- 2 tablespoons sugar

METHOD

Blend everything together in a food processor, then leave to macerate for at least a day for the flavours to mingle and the plum to liquefy before using. Store in the refrigerator for up to 3 months.

Yuzu Miso 柚子味噌

YUZU MISO

MAKES ABOUT 120 ML (4 FL OZ/½ CUP)

USE FOR Marinating or glazing oily fish, chicken or duck; or as a dip, dressing or pickling medium for vegetables.

TASTES LIKE Miso meets marmalade. Sweet, tangy, zesty.

INGREDIENTS

80 g (2¾ oz/5 heaped tablespoons) miso

2 tablespoons yuzu juice

2 tablespoons sugar

2 tablespoons mirin

METHOD

Stir all the ingredients together until well mixed and lump-free. Store in the refrigerator for up to 6 months.

Shōgayaki no Tare 生姜焼きのタレ

GINGER STIR-FRY SAUCE

MAKES ABOUT 300 ML (10 FL OZ/1¼ CUPS), ENOUGH TO MAKE 2 SIZEABLE STIR-FRIES (UP TO 6 SERVINGS TOTAL)

USE In stir-fries, especially ones with pork or crunchy veg.

TASTES Gingery and sweet, a little tangy.

INGREDIENTS

- 60 g (2 oz) fresh root ginger, peeled and sliced against the grain
- 6 tablespoons soy sauce
- 6 tablespoons mirin
- 4 tablespoons sake
- 2 tablespoons tonkatsu or Worcestershire sauce
- 1 teaspoon sesame oil

METHOD

Blend everything until smooth, then pass through a sieve (fine mesh strainer). Store in a jar or bottle in the refrigerator for up to 6 months. This sauce is better cooked out, so add it to your wok while making a stir-fry or use it to glaze meat while it's grilling or roasting. Use about 6 tablespoons for 2 servings.

MAKE IT VEGAN

Use kombu dashi powder.

Yakiniku no Tare 焼肉のタレ

JAPANESE BARBECUE SAUCE

MAKES ABOUT 300 ML (10 FL OZ/1¼ CUPS), ENOUGH FOR ABOUT 800 G (1 LB 12 OZ) MEAT, WHICH WILL SERVE 4 GENEROUSLY

USE As a marinade or dip for thinly sliced barbecued meat.

TASTES Tangy, sweet, soy saucy and a little bit fruity.

INGREDIENTS

- 120 ml (4 fl oz/½ cup) soy sauce
- 1 kiwi, peeled, or ½ small apple, peeled and cored
- 1 banana shallot, roughly chopped
- 1 small garlic clove, peeled
- 2 cm (¾ oz) fresh ginger root, peeled and thinly sliced
- 4 tablespoons mirin
- 2 tablespoons honey or light brown sugar
- 2 tablespoons rice vinegar
- 1 tablespoon sesame oil
- ¼ teaspoon black pepper

METHOD

Blitz everything in a food processor or blender until the fruit and vegetables have broken down. Use to marinate prepared meat for up to 24 hours, or as a dip for grilled meat or squid.

MAKE IT VEGAN

Replace honey with light brown sugar.

Yakitori no Tare 焼き鳥のタレ

YAKITORI SAUCE

MAKES ABOUT 150 ML (5 FL OZ/SCANT ⅔ CUP), ENOUGH FOR UP TO 20 SKEWERS

USE As a glaze for yakitori or any other grilled chicken.

TASTES Sweet, deeply savoury and a touch smoky.

INGREDIENTS

- 2 chicken wings, jointed (or about 200 g/7 oz chicken bones)
- 120 ml (4 fl oz/½ cup) soy sauce
- 1 small garlic clove, grated
- 1 cm (½ in) fresh ginger root, grated
- 4 tablespoons mirin
- 4 tablespoons sake
- 2 tablespoons honey or light brown sugar
- 2 tablespoons water
- ½ teaspoon smoked paprika

METHOD

Preheat the oven to 200°C (400°F/gas 6). Roast the chicken wings in a small casserole, or similar oven-to-stovetop cooking vessel, for 30 minutes, turning them over halfway through cooking. Set the casserole on the stovetop over a medium heat and add all of the remaining ingredients. Bring to a simmer and cook gently for about 15 minutes, until the ingredients infuse and the mixture thickens slightly. Pass through a sieve (fine mesh strainer) and store in the refrigerator for up to a month.

Nitsume 煮詰め

EEL SAUCE ☆ ❦

MAKES 100 ML (3½ FL OZ/SCANT ½ CUP), ENOUGH FOR 4 FILLETS OF FISH

USE When you need a soy sauce glaze for oily fish with a recipe that's really easy to remember.

TASTES Similar to teriyaki, but with a mellower, more balanced flavour.

INGREDIENTS

- 4 tablespoons Demerara sugar
- 4 tablespoons sake
- 4 tablespoons mirin
- 4 tablespoons soy sauce

METHOD

Tip the sugar into a saucepan and set over a medium-high heat. Cook until the sugar melts and starts to darken in spots, then add the sake and mirin. Boil the liquid for about 5 minutes to cook off the alcohol – it should reduce by about a quarter. Add the soy sauce and bring to the boil, then switch off the heat.

To use, simply brush this onto the surface of oily fish (such as mackerel or sardines) as they grill. Add multiple applications throughout cooking.

Shinpuru na Teriyaki Sōsu シンプルな照り焼きソース

TWO-INGREDIENT TERIYAKI

MAKES 150 ML (5 FL OZ/SCANT ⅔ CUP), ENOUGH FOR 4–6 SERVINGS

USE For anything grilled – especially meat, tofu and vegetables.

TASTES Punchy, straightforwardly salty-savoury-sweet, and very strong! Use just a little at first, then add more only as needed.

INGREDIENTS

6 tablespoons tamari

4 tablespoons treacle (molasses)

METHOD

Stir well, until the treacle dissolves into the tamari. This will keep at room temperature indefinitely.

Hanī Dengaku ハニー田楽

HONEY MISO

MAKES ENOUGH FOR 1 AUBERGINE, TO MAKE THE CLASSIC NASU DENGAKU (SWEET MISO-GLAZED AUBERGINE), BUT YOU CAN SCALE IT UP EASILY

USE On grilled or roasted vegetables – especially aubergine (eggplant) and tofu. Also great with lamb and salmon.

TASTES Candy-sweet, moreishly salty and surprisingly complex.

INGREDIENTS

2 tablespoons (30 g/1 oz) miso

1 tablespoon (20 g/¾ oz) honey

1 tablespoon water

METHOD

Stir all the ingredients together until well mixed and lump-free. It will keep in the refrigerator for several weeks.

Shōyu Batā 醤油バター

SOY SAUCE BUTTER ☆ ❦

MAKES 100 G (3½ OZ), ENOUGH FOR ABOUT 4 SERVINGS

USE FOR Melting over vegetables, shellfish, white fish, pasta … everything, really!

TASTES Like a perfect, complete flavour – salty, sweet, umami and rich.

INGREDIENTS

- 75 g (2½ oz/⅓ cup) unsalted butter or, very soft (it needs to be a whiskable consistency, so microwave it for a few seconds if you need to)
- 2 tablespoons soy sauce

METHOD

Whisk the soy sauce into the softened butter, little by little, until fully incorporated and smooth. Store in the refrigerator for up to 1 month.

MAKE IT VEGAN

Use plant butter.

GINGER GARLIC MISO BUTTER

MAKES 200 G (7 OZ)

USE FOR Anything – especially shellfish, sweetcorn, noodles, rice and greens.

TASTES Aromatic, salty, rich and sweet – punchy yet balanced.

INGREDIENTS

- 100 g (3½ oz/scant ½ cup) unsalted butter
- 2 garlic cloves, finely grated
- 2 cm (¾ in) chunk of fresh root ginger, finely grated
- 100 g (3½ oz/scant 7 tablespoons) miso

METHOD

Combine the butter, garlic and ginger in a small pan and set over a high heat. Melt the butter and cook for a few minutes, to soften and infuse the garlic and ginger. Leave to cool, then whisk in the miso. Store in the refrigerator for up to 3 months.

MAKE IT VEGAN

Use plant butter.

VEGAN BROCCOLI MISO PESTO ☆ ❦

MAKES ENOUGH FOR 500 G (1 LB 2 OZ) PASTA, AT LEAST 4 SERVINGS

USE In place of any normal pesto – the miso acts as an excellent replacement for both the cheese and the nuts, so it's great for vegans and people with allergies.

TASTES Like pesto!

INGREDIENTS

- 225 g (8 oz) broccoli florets (fresh or frozen)
- 30–40 g (1–1½ oz/2–2½ tablespoons) white miso
- 2–3 tablespoons olive oil, to taste
- 1 garlic clove, peeled
- 40 g (1½ oz) basil leaves (picked weight)
- 1–2 tablespoons broccoli cooking water (see method)
- salt and pepper, to taste

METHOD

Boil the broccoli until quite soft, but still bright green – about 8 minutes. Save a little of the cooking water to use in the sauce. Let the broccoli cool until no longer steaming hot, then transfer to a blender with all of the other ingredients. Blend until smooth, then taste and adjust the seasoning as you like.

MISO-MOCHI VEGAN 'CHEESE SAUCE' ❦

MAKES ABOUT 660 G (1 LB 7 OZ), ENOUGH FOR A WHOLE LASAGNE TO SERVE 6–8, OR ABOUT 6 PORTIONS OF MAC AND CHEESE

USE As a cheese sauce substitute.

TASTES More or less just like a real cheese sauce.

NOTE This recipe calls for kirimochi, dried bricks of mochi that become elastic and chewy when cooked. They have the ability to stretch, brown and congeal in a similar way to cheese, so it works really well to replicate the texture of a roux-based cheese sauce.

INGREDIENTS

- 600 ml (20 fl oz/2½ cups) unsweetened soy milk
- 3 pieces of kirimochi, cut into small cubes
- 30 g (1 oz/2 tablespoons) plant-based butter
- 80 g (2¾ oz/generous 5 tablespoons) white miso
- lemon juice, to taste
- salt, pepper, crushed garlic, ground nutmeg, nutritional yeast, vegan cream, to garnish (all optional)

METHOD

Combine the milk, kirimochi and plant-based butter in a saucepan and set over a high heat. Bring to the boil while whisking frequently and occasionally using a spatula to scrape the sides and bottom of the pan. After about 10 minutes, the kirimochi should melt and dissolve into the milk, thickening the sauce. Continue whisking until there are no more big lumps, then use a hand-held stick blender to blitz it until perfectly smooth.

Remove from the heat and blend in the miso along with a little lemon juice – start with about ½ teaspoon.

Taste and adjust the seasoning as you like. Garlic and nutmeg should be added as the sauce boils so they infuse; everything else can be added at the end of cooking. Nutritional yeast is optional, but it will really land the cheesy flavour. A glug of vegan cream at the end adds a velvety consistency and glossy finish to the sauce.

Yakisoba Sōsu 焼そばソース

YAKISOBA SAUCE

MAKES ABOUT 200 ML (7 FL OZ/SCANT 1 CUP), ENOUGH FOR 4 SERVINGS OF YAKISOBA

USE In yakisoba, or similar stir-fried noodle or vegetable dishes.

TASTES Like a slightly sweeter, richer version of Worcestershire sauce.

INGREDIENTS

- 4 tablespoons soy sauce
- 3 tablespoons Worcestershire sauce
- 4 tablespoons sake
- 2 tablespoons oyster sauce
- 2 teaspoons sugar
- ¼ teaspoon dashi powder or MSG
- white or black pepper, to taste

METHOD

Stir everything together until well mixed. Store in the refrigerator for up to 6 months.

Ankake Sōsu あんかけソース

THICK & GLOSSY DASHI SAUCE

MAKES ABOUT 300 ML (10 FL OZ/1¼ CUPS), ENOUGH FOR UP TO 4 SERVINGS

USE For pouring over stir-fries, eggs, rice and noodles – or in Nagoya, spaghetti.

TASTES Salty, umami and thick on the palate.

INGREDIENTS

- 250 ml (8 fl oz/1 cup) Katsuo Dashi (page 23)
- 2 tablespoons soy sauce
- 1 tablespoon sake
- 1 tablespoon cornflour (cornstarch) or potato starch
- 1 coin of fresh root ginger (optional)
- a few drops of sesame oil (optional)

METHOD

Whisk the dashi, soy sauce, sake and starch together in a saucepan until lump-free. Add the ginger (if using) and bring to the boil, whisking frequently, until very thick. Stir in the sesame oil at the end (if using).

Warishita 割下

SUKIYAKI SAUCE ✯ ❦

MAKES ABOUT 250 ML (8 FL OZ/1 CUP), ENOUGH FOR 4 SERVINGS, OR 2 POTS OF SUKIYAKI

USE In hotpots and rice bowls, especially ones with beef. The classic application is sukiyaki.

TASTES Very sweet, umami and salty – perfect for red meat or hearty veg.

INGREDIENTS

- 180 ml (6 fl oz/¾ cup) soy sauce
- 10 g (½ oz/about 1 tablespoon) dashi powder
- 2 tablespoons mirin
- 2 tablespoons sake
- 2 tablespoons Demerara sugar

METHOD

Combine all the ingredients in a saucepan and bring to the boil. Leave to cool and store in the refrigerator.

Use about 3 tablespoons per serving as a seasoning for rice bowls, or combine 120 ml (4 fl oz/½ cup) with 600 ml (20 fl oz/2½ cups) water to make a broth for sukiyaki or stew.

MAKE IT VEGAN

Use kombu dashi powder.

Kaeshi 返し

SOY SAUCE SEASONING FOR NOODLES ❦

MAKES ABOUT 200 ML (7 FL OZ/SCANT 1 CUP), ENOUGH FOR ABOUT 6 BOWLS OF NOODLES

USE To season dashi (or other broths) for noodles.

TASTES Mostly like soy sauce, rounded out with a little sugar and mirin.

INGREDIENTS

- 180 ml (6 fl oz/¾ cup) soy sauce
- 2 tablespoons mirin
- 1 tablespoon Demerara sugar

METHOD

Combine everything in a saucepan and bring to a bare simmer to dissolve the sugar.

Use 3–4 tablespoons per 300 ml (10 fl oz/1¼ cups) unseasoned dashi to make a bowl of broth for noodles.

Mentsuyu 麺つゆ

NOODLE SOUP BROTH CONCENTRATE ✯ ❦

MAKES ABOUT 200 ML (7 FL OZ/SCANT 1 CUP), ENOUGH FOR 4 SERVINGS OF NOODLES

USE To make a quick soup broth with just hot water, or as a dip for chilled noodles. Mixed with finely grated daikon, it can also be used as a dip for tempura.

TASTES Strongly of dashi and soy sauce, with a touch of sweetness.

INGREDIENTS

- 180 ml (6 fl oz/¾ cup) soy sauce
- 10 g (½ oz/about 1 tablespoon) dashi powder
- 2 tablespoons mirin
- 1 tablespoon Demerara sugar

METHOD

Combine everything in a small saucepan and bring to the boil to dissolve the sugar. Leave to cool. Store in the refrigerator for up to 3 months.

To use, dilute 45–50 ml (1½–1¾ fl oz/ 3–3½ tablespoons) mentsuyu into 300 ml (10 fl oz/1¼ cups) hot water. Halve the amount of water to make a dip for chilled noodles.

MAKE IT VEGAN

Use kombu dashi powder.

Ninniku Miso Goma Dare にんにく味噌胡麻ダレ

GARLIC MISO SESAME DRESSING ✯ ❦

MAKES 200 ML (7 FL OZ/SCANT 1 CUP), ABOUT 8 SERVINGS

USE As a dressing for chilled noodles, or a dip for anything that can take strong, rich flavours. Good with brassicas, mangetout (snow peas) or any crunchy, peppery leaves.

TASTES Nutty, garlicky, complex and addictive.

INGREDIENTS

- 3 tablespoons sesame seeds
- 3 tablespoons tahini
- 3 tablespoons miso
- 2 tablespoons mirin
- 2 tablespoons rice vinegar
- 2 tablespoons sugar
- 2 tablespoons sesame oil
- 1½ tablespoons vegetable oil
- ½ teaspoon hot mustard (English or Japanese)
- ¼ teaspoon MSG
- 2–3 garlic cloves, peeled
- 1–3 tablespoons water
- salt, as needed (optional)

METHOD

Tip the sesame seeds into a frying pan and set over a medium-high heat. Toast the sesame seeds, stirring often, for about 8 minutes until bronzed. Remove from the pan and leave to cool.

Transfer the sesame seeds to a blender or food processor and blend to a fine, sandy texture, then add all of the remaining ingredients and blend until smooth. If you want this to be a thinner, more pourable consistency, add a little more water, then taste and adjust the seasoning as needed with salt.

Store in the refrigerator for up to 2 weeks.

WORKS REFERENCED

INTRODUCTION

p.7 Erdal, M. 2025, 'Melek Erdal's İçli Köfte Two Ways (One Disrespectful)', *Vittles*: www.vittlesmagazine.com/p/melek-erdals-icli-kofte-two-ways

THE F WORD

p.9 Lau, J., *An A–Z of Chinese Food*, (Renegade Books, 2025)

p.11 Johnson, R. M., *Small Fires* (ONE, 2022)

CHAPTER 1
KOMBU AND KATSUOBUSHI

ja.wikipedia.org/wiki/□□□#□□

ja.wikipedia.org/wiki/□□#□□

thejapanesefoodlab.com/katsuobushi-making/

www.instagram.com/takashi_tamari/p/DKUc5GhtTNK/?hl=en

www.koikeya-online.jp/shop/g/g17916-c/

www.ndl.go.jp/kaleido/entry/17/2.html

P.30: FURIKAKE-CURED SALMON

Maehashi, N. 2017, 'Cured Salmon Gravlax', recipetineats: https://www.recipetineats.com/cured-salmon-gravlax/

P.32: FURIKAKE FOCACCIA

Graves, H., *BBQ Days BBQ Nights* (Hardie Grant UK, 2024)

CHAPTER 2
MISO

Belleme, J. and J., *The Miso Book* (Square One Publishing, 2004)

Chung, B., *Miso Tasty* (Pavilion Books, 2016)

Chung, B., *Miso*: *From Japanese Classics to Everyday Umami* (Pavilion Books, 2026)

Morimoto, K., *Ferment* (One Boat, 2025)

Shurtleff, W. and Aoyagi, A., *The Book of Miso* (1976)

P.39: MISOSTRONE

www.bbcgoodfood.com/recipes/classic-minestrone-soup

P.44: HIPSTER HISPI

Rayner, J., *Nights Out at Home* (Fig Tree, 2024)

P.49: WAFŪ RAREBIT

Cloake, F. 2011, 'How to Cook Perfect Welsh Rarebit', *The Guardian*: www.theguardian.com/lifeandstyle/wordofmouth/2011/oct/27/how-to-cook-perfect-welsh-rarebit

P.50: CHICKEN MEATLOAF

www.kurashiru.com/recipes/13bdc042-0de6-4c35-9975-885469932efc

www.netflix.com/watch/81760357

www.yukigomi.com/blog/miso-chicken-recipe/

www.yutori.co.jp/shop/rp/rp160515/

P.56: NO-CHURN MISO ICE CREAM

www.bbcgoodfood.com/recipes/no-churn-ice-cream

CHAPTER 3
SOY SAUCE

Iino, R., 'The History of Shoyu (Soy Sauce)', Kikkoman.com: www.kikkoman.com/jp/kiifc/foodculture/pdf_01/e_012_015.pdf

ja.wikipedia.org/wiki/醤油

www.soysauce.or.jp/faq/about-others

P.74: SOY SAUCE AND SHICHIMI GUINNESS CAKE

Domestic Gothess.com 2022, 'Vegan Guinness Chocolate Cake': domesticgothess.com/blog/2022/08/22/vegan-guinness-chocolate-cake/

donalskehan.com/recipes/chocolate-guinness-cake/

CHAPTER 4
SAKE, MIRIN AND RICE VINEGAR

www.instagram.com/p/DDkA0gOOsmU/?img_index=5&igsh=eW!1b3NiZnBraDF3
en.wikipedia.org/wiki/Rice_vinegar

P.83: CHINESE-JAPANESE FRIED AUBERGINE WITH TANGY LEEK SAUCE

ja.wikipedia.org/wiki/油淋鶏

www.justonecookbook.com/fried-chicken-with-scallion-soy-sauce/

www.kurashiru.com/recipes/073888e6-5e68-4e5c-9ef7-d77d70de453e

www.maangchi.com/recipe/yuringi

P.86: SCAMPI IN THE STYLE OF KATSUDON

www.katauoya.com/

「カツ丼」の基本レシピをプロが伝授！とろふわにするコツも必見 – macaroni

https://macaro-ni.jp/65847

CHAPTER 5
RICE AND NOODLES

p.97: Ohnuki-Tierney, E., *Rice as Self* (Princeton University Press, 1993)

www.komenet.jp/bunkatorekishi/

www.jstor.org/stable/j.ctt7t91m

www.nippon.com/en/japan-topics/g00940/

note.com/coto_11/n/n530d8d8c75bc

ja.wikipedia.org/wiki/うどん#歴史

P.103: 'ASIAN' SLAW

sandygoe.substack.com/p/sumi-salad-moms-legacy-goes-global

CHAPTER 6
TOFU

ja.wikipedia.org/wiki/豆腐#日本の豆腐

www.tofu-as.com/english/tofu/howto/03.html

P.124: TOFU MISO KATSU

www.kurashiru.com/recipes/06e79958-53d5-4078-ba72-0e2abfbe4cf5

P.134: TOFUMISO

schoolnightvegan.com/home/vegan-ladyfingers/#recipe

CHAPTER 7
YUZU JUICE, PONZU & YUZU KOSHŌ

www.sciencedirect.com/science/article/abs/pii/S030881460801474X

CHAPTER 8
CURRY ROUX

Rath, E., p.144: *Japan's Cuisines* (Reaktion Books, 2016)

P.167: SWEET AND SPICY CURRY WINGS

tastesbetterfromscratch.com/crispy-baked-chicken-wings/

CHAPTER 9
TEA AND OTHER BEVERAGES

pmc.ncbi.nlm.nih.gov/articles/PMC6213777/

www.theguardian.com/food/2025/apr/05/skyrocketing-demand-for-matcha-raises-fears-of-shortage-in-japan

P.175: VEGAN MATCHA-MISO DOUBLE CHEESECAKE

Khoury, P., *A New Way to Bake* (Hardie Grant UK, 2023)

P.180: GRASSHOPPER

suebeehomemaker.com/frozen-grasshoppers/#recipe

CHAPTER 10
THE LIBRARY OF CONDIMENTS

P.200: JAPANESE TARTARE SAUCE

www.gakkyludique.com/entry/tartar_source

macaro-ni.jp/49282

P.205: SOUR PLUM MISO

www.orangepage.net/recipes/detail_122811#google_vignette

www.kyounoryouri.jp/recipe/603590_梅みそ.html

oceans-nadia.com/user/146865/recipe/420438

www.justonecookbook.com/ume-miso/

P.205: SOY SAUCE PICKLE BRINE

www.instagram.com/kenjcooks/reel/CxxO6G_oZY-/

P.209: EEL SAUCE

kinarino.jp/cat4/43931

P.213: MISO-MOCHI VEGAN 'CHEESE SAUCE'

cookpad.com/jp/recipes/17795256-切り餅ホットミルクホワイトソース

www.hotpepper.jp/mesitsu/entry/nishitamao/2021-00687

ACKNOWLEDGEMENTS

Thank you thank you thank you to everyone who makes these books! In no particular order: Holly Arnold, Eila Purvis, Judith Hannam, Kajal Mistry, Patricia Niven, Tamara Vos, Aya Nishimura, Evi O, Emily Preece-Morrison and a whole bunch of other people who work behind the scenes at Quadrille! Also to food world folks including George Egg, Helen Graves, Fumio Tanga, Gurd Loyal, Melissa Thompson, Melek Erdal, Rebecca May Johnson, Laura Goodman, Jenny Lau, Jay Rayner, Zoe Laughlin, Barry Smith, Catherine Phipps, James Chant, Kenji Morimoto, Maunika Gowardhan, Shelina Permaloo, Anna Ansari, Su Scott, Uyen Luu, MiMi Aye, Akemi Yokoyama, Yuki Gomi, Owen Barratt, Janine Ratcliffe, Morgan Pitelka, Patrick Knill, Aaron Vallance, Philip Khoury, Tim Kinnaird, Amy Sheppard, Atsuko Ikeda, Kavita Favelle, Nic Miller, Florentyna Leow, Matt Curtis, Esther Clark, and many many others who have inspired, educated and/or supported me in all sorts of ways over the years!

Finally, thank you to Laura, Tig and Felix, for always being open-minded and appreciative* guinea pigs and for bringing me joy in a world that feels hell-bent on delivering nothing but despair. I love you all.

*(Laura only)

ABOUT THE AUTHOR

Tim Anderson is a Wisconsin-born, London-based writer who has pursued an interest in Japanese food for 25 years. He has previously written eight books on Japanese cookery, including *Hokkaido*, *Ramen Forever*, *Your Home Izakaya* and the *JapanEasy* series. He also writes about Midwestern American food and the death of the American dream on his Substack, *24 Hour Pancake People*.

INDEX

Quadrille, Penguin Random House UK,
One Embassy Gardens, 8 Viaduct Gardens, London SW11 7BW

Quadrille Publishing Limited is part of the Penguin Random House group of companies whose addresses can be found at global.penguinrandomhouse.com

Published by Quadrille in 2026

www.penguin.co.uk

A CIP catalogue record for this book is available from the British Library

ISBN 978-1-83783-454-9
10 9 8 7 6 5 4 3 2 1

Managing Director, Publishing: Sarah Lavelle
Publishing Director: Kajal Mistry
Senior Editor: Eila Purvis
Designer: Evi-O.Studio
Photographer: Patricia Niven
Photography assistant: Sam Neeves
Props stylist: Aya Nishimura
Food stylist: Tamara Vos
Copy-editor: Emily Preece-Morrison
Proofreader: Clare Double
Indexer: Cathy Heath
Production Manager: Sabeena Atchia

Colour reproduction by p2d

Printed in China by C&C Offset Printing Co., Ltd.

The authorised representative in the EEA is
Penguin Random House Ireland, Morrison Chambers, 32 Nassau Street, Dublin D02 YH68.

Penguin Random House is committed to a sustainable future for our business, our readers and our planet. This book is made from Forest Stewardship Council® certified paper.

さようなら